Against Affect

SERIES EDITORS · *Marco Abel and Roland Végső*

PROV
OCAT
IONS

Something in the world forces us to think.
—Gilles Deleuze

The world provokes thought. Thinking is nothing but the human response to this provocation. Thus, the very nature of thought is to be the product of a provocation. This is why a genuine act of provocation cannot be the empty rhetorical gesture of the contrarian. It must be an experimental response to the historical necessity to act. Unlike the contrarian, we refuse to reduce provocation to a passive noun or a state of being. We believe that real moments of provocation are constituted by a series of actions that are best defined by verbs or even infinitives—verbs in a modality of potentiality, of the promise of action. To provoke is to intervene in the present by invoking an as yet undecided future radically different from what is declared to be possible in the present and, in so doing, to arouse the desire for bringing about change. By publishing short books from multiple disciplinary perspectives that are closer to the genres of the manifesto, the polemical essay, the intervention, and the pamphlet than to traditional scholarly monographs, "Provocations" hopes to serve as a forum for the kind of theoretical experimentation that we consider to be the very essence of thought.

www.provocationsbooks.com

Against Affect

LISA DOWNING

UNIVERSITY OF NEBRASKA PRESS · LINCOLN

© 2026 by the Board of Regents of
the University of Nebraska

All rights reserved

The University of Nebraska Press is part
of a land-grant institution with campuses
and programs on the past, present, and
future homelands of the Pawnee, Ponca,
Otoe-Missouria, Omaha, Dakota, Lakota,
Kaw, Cheyenne, and Arapaho Peoples,
as well as those of the relocated Ho-
Chunk, Sac and Fox, and Iowa Peoples.

For customers in the EU with safety/
GPSR concerns, contact:
gpsr@mare-nostrum.co.uk
Mare Nostrum Group BV
Mauritskade 21D
1091 GC Amsterdam
The Netherlands

Library of Congress Cataloging-in-Publication
Data can be found at search.catalog.loc.gov:

ISBN 978-1-4962-4230-3 (paperback)

Set in Sorts Mill Goudy by Lacey Losh.
Designed by N. Putens.

CONTENTS

Acknowledgments   vii

Provocations   ix

Introduction   1

1. Repairing What Wasn't Broken:
   Queer Theory's Affective Turn   27

2. Why Aren't We Minding Our Own Shoes?
   On Empathy   43

3. Words as Weapons:
   The Tyranny of Vulnerability   67

4. If Reason Went Viral:
   Rethinking Vulnerability in COVID-19 Culture   95

   Conclusion:
   For a Feminist Neo-Enlightenment   117

   Notes   131

ACKNOWLEDGMENTS

The contribution and support of many individuals and organizations must be acknowledged here. Firstly, I am immensely grateful to the Leverhulme Trust for the award of a Leverhulme Research Fellowship in 2021 that enabled me to carry out a large part of the research for, and writing of, this book while staying at home and shielding from COVID-19. I like to think the Leverhulme kept me uninfected as well as giving me space and time to write. My referees for the Leverhulme Fellowship, Peter Cryle, Laura Doan, and Emma Wilson, are owed a particular note of gratitude.

For kindly providing me with platforms and opportunities to present, share, and receive feedback on the ideas in *Against Affect*, thanks are due to Oliver Davis and colleagues at the University of Warwick; Stephen Forcer and colleagues at the University of Glasgow; Ben Nichols, Elliot Evans, and the AHRC-funded research network "Beyond Radical: Queer Theory and the UK"; Rebecca Wynter, Manon Parry, Andries Hiskes, Kristine Johanson, and their colleagues at UVA, the Netherlands; and Nadia Jones-Gailani, Erzsébet Barát, and their colleagues at CEU, Vienna, Austria.

Other colleagues and friends with whom I've debated, discussed, developed, and defended these arguments—and without whom this book could not have come to fruition—include, but are by no means limited to: Miranda Gill, Robert Gillett, Mary Harrod, Katharina Karcher, Jules O'Dwyer, Maria Scott, Elizabeth Stephens, Michael Syrotinski, Ingrid Wassenaar, Andrew Watts, Susannah Wilson, and the "Empathy-Critical" research team in Mental Health Humanities at my home institution, the University of Birmingham. I owe a debt to Keidrick Roy who kindly shared with me the pre-publication proof of his monograph *Dark Age*, which was influential for my argument in parts of this book.

I'd like to thank the "Provocations" series editors at the University of Nebraska Press, Marco Abel and Roland Végso, for their intellectual vision and for the trust they place in their authors, and acquisitions editor Courtney Ochsner for her efficiency and kindness throughout. Finally, to the two external readers, Walter Benn Michaels and a reader who wishes to remain anonymous, immense thanks are due for their detailed and engaged responses which helped me to strengthen the book's arguments.

PROVOCATIONS

The language of emotion is historically gendered and racialized to the detriment of women, people of color, and other nonnormative subjects. Affect theory has elevated emotion and feeling in both the academy and in contemporary culture to the degree that prioritizing them has become not only the hegemonic norm, but also a strategy that is cynically deployed in the service of exercising power. The duty to put emotions and feelings first has led to a climate of authoritarian censoriousness and self-censorship that it is now time to challenge. Asking why affect theory chose to revalorize feeling rather than redistribute reason, I claim that:

- If the ideal of reason were not the better, more productive, more pleasurable virtue, the eighteenth-century Enlightened patriarch would not have claimed it for himself as the proper condition of maleness.
- Being able to "stand in someone else's shoes" (empathy) is not morally superior to deciding rationally to stand "alongside" them (solidarity).
- We must resist the Tyranny of Vulnerability.

- We must not permit any set of ideas to be off-limits for legitimate critique; squeamish leftist denials of the existence of a "culture war" simply cede the ground of defining the terms of that war to the right.
- A commitment to recognizing that feelings are real, powerful, and inevitable must not prevent our urgent critique of the use of emotive language for propagandist ends.
- It is better to redistribute reason than to revalorize affect.
- A reinstatement of the values of freedom of expression (however hurtful) and reason as an ideal (if not always a perfectly executable one) are the necessary conditions for liberty, compassion, and respect.
- As the most effective redress to the failed affective turn, we need to imagine and work toward a Feminist Neo-Enlightenment.

Against Affect

Introduction

Is there any remaining doubt that we are now
fully within the Episteme of the Affect?
—Eugenie Brinkema, *The Forms of the Affects*

We must try to proceed with the analysis of ourselves
as beings who are historically determined, to a
certain extent, by the Enlightenment.
—Michel Foucault, "What is Enlightenment?"

Although Kant said some very stupid things about women,
reason is not a masculine construction. Rather, partly because
Kant wrote, reason is ours, a universal present in everyone.
—Margaret C. Jacob, "The Mental Landscape of
the Public Sphere: A European Perspective"

In this book I want to ask a number of questions about what it might mean to declare oneself "against affect," where "affect" is understood in a very specific sense, a sense that is directly related to the academic "affective turn," but that also moves beyond it into all areas of public and political discursive life. I shall also bring critical attention to the notion of being "against," which I intend in a more nuanced and less absolutist way than outright rejection. I invite the reader to understand the "against" of my title provocatively and provisionally as a challenge to think reflexively about what we assume to be "good" and "bad" in value—and what it might mean to argue *contra* what passes as an unmarked good at a particular moment in cultural history. The invitation to be (provisionally) against affect is an invitation to think against the grain about the ethical and epistemological underpinnings of taking emotion or feeling as the best way of apprehending and inviting responses to the world, to political situations, and to others. For this proposition to make sense, it would need to be understood that affect is currently the dominant episteme in our twenty-first-century cultural moment, as Eugenie Brinkema rhetorically proposes in the first quotation of my epigraph, threatening to eclipse the episteme of Enlightenment that shaped us as moderns, according to Michel Foucault in the second. And that is one of the claims that this book will elaborate and demonstrate. A further claim it will make is that this state of affairs is not necessarily a desirable one.

The aim throughout my book, as should be obvious, is not to oppose or discourage the feeling of emotions themselves in any literal sense, for individuals or for the collective—that would be as impossible a demand to make as it would be undesirable. Nor do I believe, in the face of evidence from the cognitive, psychiatric, and neurological sciences, that it is genuinely possible to separate thinking from feeling, body from mind, experientially, in any absolutist way. The research of neuroscientist Antonio Damasio has shown that emotions are in fact inherently "enmeshed" in the "networks" of reason.[1] Instead, I consider the fraught pair of "feeling" and "reason" as *discursive terms, positions, or rhetorics* in political, cultural, and academic life that undoubtedly still resonate and obtain, long after the questioning of Cartesian dualism, and that operate as a cultural and philosophical pair—with different weight attributed to them in different historical moments. Indeed, the history of separating reason from feeling and opposing them to each other as a pair is long and checkered. We find it in Plato with the notion of the "tripartite soul" comprising reason, appetite, and spirit as distinct parts. We find it in the metaphysics of Descartes, with the primacy of thought as the ontological prerequisite for being human (the "cogito"). And it is, of course, a pair of ideas central to the Enlightenment—that contested and complex phenomenon that I shall discuss in the next section of this introduction.

Jacques Derrida's deconstruction has taught us much about the enduringness of binary thinking, and also about the necessity of recognizing the power imbalances that inhere in it. In this tradition, in *Matter, Affect, Antinormativity: Theory Beyond Dualism* (2022), which attempts to avoid thinking "for" or "against" a series of binary pairs for politically progressive ends, Caroline Braunmühl argues that privileging either "affect" or "discourse" involves colluding in "unegalitarian (gendered, racialized) discourses that are implicated in sustaining social inequality."[2] She proposes instead thinking about feeling and discourse as "*mutually implicating, yet irreducible to one another.*"[3] It is self-evident that these terms coexist in a relationship of tension. I depart from Braunmühl in that I do not necessarily agree that demonstrating how one term in a binary may speak more appropriately or powerfully to a given situation or moment inevitably replicates the historical inequality built into hierarchal binaries—unless we assume that making any value judgment on the basis of any evidence is always already an oppressive act. In this vein I should emphasize here that my critique of affect is time-and-place-specific. I argue that a commitment to recognizing that feeling is real, powerful, important, and inevitable must not prevent our urgent critique of the use of emotive language for the purposes of coercive cultural propaganda. And I question the notion that the broad turn from a prioritization of reason or critical thinking ("Enlightenment thinking") to a prioritization of affective responses and a reliance on "experience," in relation to culture, to political events, and to the other, has been a wholly positive or progressive move.

As noted, binaries established as such over time that may not be "true," in the sense of being epistemologically or ontologically defensible, nevertheless persist in the cultural imaginary, shaping how we think and organize knowledge and affecting our judgments. It is precisely how the obstinate pair "reason" and "feeling" are deployed, valorized, and set against each other in the current moment that interests me here. As we look around us, we may find evidence that a cultural imperative such as "Be reasonable! Think critically!" has been replaced by exhortations such as "Be kind! Words are literal violence!" or, conversely, "Be proud of your traditions! Protect Western values! Make America great again!" This binary pair of sets of exhortations exemplifies another keystone of my book's claims: that the lexical field of "feeling" and appeals to emotion are being deployed by what we might traditionally think of as both left-wing and right-wing causes. Though, I would also add here that the terms "left" and "right" increasingly lose their fixed meanings, with other terms such as *populism, nationalism, authoritarianism, libertarianism, wokeism,* and *identitarianism,* among others, describing more saliently contemporary political trends. Indeed, the fact that it is possible to identify a creep of the language of feeling in discourses issuing from all points on the political compass suggests that what I will call the "cultural affective turn" (an offspring of its academic counterpart) is a broad and prevalent discursive and imaginative phenomenon. I will analyze as case studies some examples of this trend from both political "sides" of what is sometimes termed a "culture war" in chapter 3 of this book.

A further underpinning premise of this book is that the

language of emotion and reason is historically gendered and racialized in ways that demand destabilization. This is because, since the Enlightenment project of the eighteenth century, women and people of color have been associated with emotionality and white men with logic and reason, with the latter elevated above the former, regardless of the capacities of all subjects. The affective turn marked an attempt to challenge this historical bias, but it did this by prioritizing the previously deprecated affective field, marked as the "feminine," rather than by challenging the ascription of attributes such as reason to subjects in a meaningful way—as Margaret Jacob suggests is wholly necessary, in the third quotation of the epigraph. It is in this context that I seek to interrogate the efficacy of the affective turn and to think about alternative ways of redressing historical prejudices.

The Age of Reason: The Enlightenment and Its Critics

This section sets out a history of our philosophical understanding of reason and feeling as distinct from each other and examines the gendering and racialization of these ideas in the context of the Enlightenment or "Age of Reason"—with the concomitant historical valuation of supposed white, masculine reason over racialized, feminine feeling.

The term "Enlightenment" is a contested and slippery one, and I do not have space here to do full justice to the depth and breadth of differing characterizations and interpretations of it. Suffice it to set out some parameters: In historical terms, there is no consensus regarding its duration, with some historians writing of a "long Enlightenment" stretching from the 1690s to the end of the eighteenth century—or even the early nineteenth century.[4] In terms of its cultural and intellectual character, several writers have insisted that Enlightenment phenomena differ depending on time and geographical location, with localized distinctions between the varied countries of Europe and the United States.[5] It is not a philosophical or social monolith; rather it is characterized by "myriad contrasting visions of morality and politics."[6] Dorinda Outram has termed the Enlightenment "a *capsule* containing sets of debates, stresses and concerns,"[7] developing directly Peter Gay's claim in his canonical two-volume study published in 1966 and 1969 that we would do better to think of Enlightenment not as a system of thought or a "moment" but as an intellectual "mood."[8] Picking up on its central imagery of light (the light of reason that is cast on the shadows of ignorance), Genevieve Lloyd has explored the shadowy underside of Enlightenment, its pessimism as well as its optimism, its emotion as well as its reason, and the ghostly quality of an *ideal* of reason that not only haunts our present imaginings of that past "mood", but that, back in the eighteenth century, took the form of "tentative ideas" that were projected "wistfully towards the future."[9] As uncontroversially as possible, we might say that some agreed-upon qualities of Enlightenment philosophy and society include: a focus upon rationality and rationalism and a rejection of superstition, the establishment of a public sphere, personal freedom and the rise of the individual, and a social contract–based understanding of society.

It is a commonplace to acknowledge that the praxis known as Modern Critical Theory that rose to academic fashion in the 1980s, with its focus on the instability of the subject, the relativization of truth claims, and the exposure of the workings of power underpinning systems of supposed objectivity, embodied suspicion of the ideal of rational thinking bequeathed to us by the Enlightenment, and attempted to execute a debunking of them. Inspiring such critiques was *Dialectic of Enlightenment* (1944) by the Frankfurt school's Max Horkheimer and Theodor W. Adorno. Herein, they argue that the value the Enlightenment had placed on science and the human capacity for reason had failed to deliver cultural flourishing, giving rise instead to forms of tyranny and domination. The book's publication date, during the darkest days of World War II, can explain some of the despair and disillusionment it expresses. *Dialectic* also argues that the attempted rejection of superstition in favor of reason was flawed, since the Enlightenment simply resulted in new forms of mythmaking—with reason as the new object of faith. Yet even within their profound critique, there is the sense that Enlightenment ideals themselves—while never foolproof—were not programmatically doomed to fail, but that their contingent manipulation by bad actors led to the dismal outcomes of their contemporaneous moment. Moreover Horkheimer, writing on "Reason Against Itself: Some Remarks on Enlightenment" in 1946, notes that it is incumbent upon us to "encourage Enlightenment to move forward even in the face of its most paradoxical consequences... The hope of Reason lies in the emancipation from its own fear of despair."[10]

In his published lecture "The 'World' of the Enlightenment to Come" (2003), Derrida asks about the conditions that would be necessary to "save the honor of reason."[11] Herein he undertakes a reading of phenomenological thinker Edmund Husserl's refusal to rehabilitate what Derrida calls "a certain Enlightenment and a certain rationalism," on the grounds of Husserl's insistence that it is founded on an idea of science that is incapable of standing against the tide of irrationality visible on the European continent in the 1930s.[12] Derrida asserts that, by being insufficiently anchored to ethical commitment, this version of reason renders itself irredeemable for Husserl. Derrida, however, does not propose doing away with the ideal of rationality, rather he sees reason, here and throughout his work, in the words of one critic, as a "a self-reflexive critique" that is as indispensable as it is imperfect.[13] He calls for a renewed thinking of reason or of what is reasonable—a tarrying with "a reason [that] must let itself be reasoned with" as central to a project of ethics.[14]

Another thinker with a critical, if ambivalent, relationship with reason—and who will be especially influential for some of my arguments in this book—is philosopher and historian Michel Foucault, whose early work on madness and reason, and later essays on Enlightenment thinking, especially that of Immanuel Kant, are particularly pertinent. The view Foucault holds of reason is hard to pin down, mainly because it develops and changes at different moments in his writing trajectory. Perhaps with a nod to this, Foucault quips in an interview in 1982: "I had been mad enough to study reason; I was reasonable enough to study madness."[15]

Foucault's earliest writing on the subject focused on the question of insanity as a form of deprivileged knowledge. *Folie et déraison: histoire de la folie à l'âge classique* (1961), first translated into English in very abridged form in 1965 as *Madness and Civilization: A History of Insanity in the Age of Reason*, and published in full in English in 2006, traces the discourses of reason and unreason from the Middle Ages to the present day in Western Europe. Foucault's principal argument here is that "folly" and reason, once understood as existing in an intertwined relationship of balance, have been separated and estranged from each other with the dawn of the Enlightenment and then modernity, via a decisive "act of scission."[16] Drawing on figures such as the counterintuitively wise Shakespearean fool and the imagery of the Ship of Fools, a vessel full of madmen who set sail in search of the secrets of their own—and the world's—wisdom, Foucault makes the claim that pre-Enlightenment societies held a place and a value for "the mad." He suggests that their role was to navigate the gap between order and chaos on behalf of the whole society. A major shift occurred, according to Foucault, in the middle of the seventeenth century, when the mad were contained in asylums that were "semi-juridical" institutions, and then, later, a second shift occurred with the efflorescence of psychiatric medicine in the nineteenth century. Psychiatry freed the mad from literal shackles, hence its legacy as a liberalizing force, but transformed them into "patients" who existed in a perpetual power relationship with doctor figures. The Enlightenment's institutions that promised to free us from religious domination and superstitious fear appear in this reading mainly as instruments of control. The historical accuracy of elements of Foucault's broad brushstroke account of the history of madness has been called into question,[17] but the picture that he paints of the narrowing of the field of reason and its exclusion of other forms of knowing remains a resonant one. Yet, when Foucault turns his attention to Kant, decades later, his approach to the question of reason is rather different.

In 1784, writing in the *Berlinische Monatsschrift*, under the title "Was ist Aufklärung?" ("What is Enlightenment?"), Kant defined Enlightenment as the cultural moment and mode in which human beings became possessed of the freedom to make public use of their reason in order to liberate humankind from cowardly immaturity. Kant proposed "*Sapere Aude*," usually translated as "Dare to know" or "Have the courage to use your own conviction" as the slogan of Enlightenment thinking. Foucault wrote a number of reflections on Kant and Enlightenment, most famously his identically entitled essay "Qu'est-ce que les lumières" or "What is Enlightenment?," produced in 1984—exactly two centuries after the publication of Kant's piece.[18] In this essay, Foucault argues that Enlightenment is the mode of thinking that gives rise to "a permanent critique of our historical era."[19]

I am reminded in posing my challenge of *thinking against affect* of Foucault's words regarding "thinking against": "One does not have to be 'for' or 'against' the Enlightenment. . . .

precisely . . . one must refuse everything that might present itself in the form of a simplistic and authoritarian alternative: you either accept the Enlightenment and remain within the tradition of its rationalism (this is considered a positive term by some and used by others, on the contrary, as a reproach), or else you criticize the Enlightenment and try to escape from its principles of rationality (which may be seen once again as good or bad)."[20] One of the reasons that Foucault suggests as to why we cannot be wholly for or against the notion of Enlightenment is that it is not possible to extract ourselves from our locatedness in precisely a post-Enlightenment European tradition of thinking, as it is the cultural-intellectual air we breathe. Looked at in another way, Foucault suggests that the very project of being able to question the Enlightenment is, to some extent, potentiated by our being its heirs.

Foucault further argues that "we must free ourselves from the intellectual blackmail of being 'for or against the Enlightenment,'"[21] and he states that we cannot avoid this "by introducing 'dialectical' nuances."[22] I want to avoid this same either-or thinking that Foucault describes with regard to the Enlightenment when trying to evaluate affect, but I also have more time for "dialectical nuances" than Foucault does. Indeed, in places, especially in the conclusion, I will apply a kind of dialectical thinking strategically, as a way of avoiding the unhelpful absolutist gesture of rejection or adherence, and also as a way of acknowledging that we have historically passed beyond the point of straightforwardly choosing either "Enlightenment episteme" or "affective episteme," since we have lived through and been shaped by both of their domains. I should caveat this by saying that I agree with Foucault's position that because the Enlightenment has both permitted and conditioned a certain mode of critical questioning our critique of it is therefore *in and of itself* an exercise of Enlightenment-infused thinking. I do not, however, believe that the affective turn has yet issued in *quite* so fundamental a sea change that we cannot operate outside of it at all—although there are attempts to have it work like this, and the price of questioning these totalizing attempts can be a particular flavor of vitriol issuing from its adherents.

One of the main challenges of reviving an Enlightenment "mood" for our age, as a counterpoint to the tsunami of affect we find ourselves under, is precisely that Enlightenment thinking in its original day excluded so many subjects from its remit. In the introduction to *Race and the Enlightenment: A Critical Reader*, editor Emmanuel Chukwude Eze notes that the classification of human beings into races is itself a product of the Enlightenment and that, like classical Greek thought, Enlightenment thinking tended to order the world between Western (European) civilization as the seat of reason and everywhere else as tarnished by barbarism.[23] He also points out the failure of many commentators—including Foucault, Hannah Arendt, and others—when writing on the key names of Enlightenment (Kant, Hume, et al.) to account for the derogatory accounts of people of color in their "minor" writings, which are often passed over as of little philosophical significance, despite what they tell us about historical-cultural attitudes that are of import.[24]

Historian Barbara Taylor, who carried out a major research project on feminism and the transnational Enlightenment in the 1990s, has noted that the Enlightenment "has been caricatured as a white-male-bourgeois scramble for power masked in a duplicitous discourse of universal emancipation"—a view she describes as "simplistic."[25] Similarly, Margaret Jacob has argued that the Enlightenment "put women's rights on the Western agenda just as it augured all the other struggles about the meaning and truthfulness of democratic practices with which we still live."[26] She further contends that the Enlightenment's creation of the "public sphere," theorized by Jürgen Habermas, did not in all national contexts create a programmatically masculine sphere, but also provided a public square for women. These feminist historical scholars suggest that women's freedoms were potentiated by Enlightenment understandings of the individual and their universal rights, even as some of its key thinkers displayed dismaying attitudes toward women's capabilities. Taylor writes: "The Enlightenment world resisted feminist ideas as much as it encouraged their emergence,"[27] offering the examples of Jean-Jacques Rousseau's followers opposing campaigns for female equality and the Jacobins moving to close down women's clubs. And she draws attention to the way in which Kant's "modernist liberal stance"[28] did not prevent his negative position on women's rights, considering the exercise of rational critique a danger for women owing to their supposedly delicate, caring, and fragile constitutions. All of these instances draw attention to the Enlightenment's "universalist assumptions about the nature of Man which had complex and often contradictory implications for notions about Woman."[29]

The question we need to grapple with here, then, is the thorny one of whether racism and sexism are a *feature* or a *bug* of the Enlightenment style of thinking—and also whether this kind of anachronism (demanding that movements of the past have the values of the present) is even helpful. If one assumes the former, its recoverability for women and people of color appears at first to be limited. Yet this absolutist purism and lack of pragmatism would appear to me to limit our horizons. Suffrage in England, for example, was designed originally only for those subjects deemed capable of it—land-owning white men. Yet the prejudice regarding who was fit to be included did not prevent socialist and feminist movements from pursuing robust fights to expand the bandwidth of citizens deemed fit to vote, rather than arguing that *nobody* should vote. This example is one of asserting the universal *potential* of concepts that are problematically ascribed, in line with the spirited quotation from Margaret Jacob that serves as my third epigraph quotation. Reason should be, in relation to Kant's stupidity regarding woman's capacity for it, as the baby is to the bathwater. Also, it must be noted that women and people of color were themselves the authors of Enlightenment projects, even if their achievements often go unrecognized in the canons that have persevered, with a very few exceptions. (Mary Wollstonecraft is perhaps the single Enlightenment woman thinker who would commonly be cited in popular canons.)

In this revisionist spirit, Surya Parekh argues in *Black Enlightenment* (2022) for the key contribution of Black intellectuals to the Enlightenment project, from positions that are heterogeneous and transformational. Focusing particularly on the examples of Francis Williams, Ignatius Sancho, and poet Phillis Wheatley, all Black authors in Britain or the British colonies, Parekh shows how the writings of these names demonstrated the impossibility of the coexistence of slavery and morality in ways that were profoundly influential, even as their import was only partially recognized in explicit terms, and their legacies incompletely archived. In his posthumously published *Letters* (1782), for example, Sancho identified the project of abolition "with Enlightenment and Christianity," writing how abolitionist tracts should "produce remorse" for the "enlightened white reader."[30] Parekh claims that "The Black subject undoes the philosophical equilibrium of a Hume or Kant," and demonstrates how the individual Black writers in question constructed contemporaneous and alternative versions of Enlightenment to show up the ethical aporia of the grand narrative.[31]

Also working in this urgent emergent field, intellectual historian Keidrick Roy, in his doctoral dissertation that undertook to assess the legacy of Black Enlightenment writers for the present, has argued that "To ignore the ways that Black writers remade the Enlightenment into a usable philosophy is to accept the inequality, unrest, and polarization we face today."[32] And in his book, *American Dark Age* (2024), Roy explores how some African Americans adopted and developed a movement of liberalism—what Roy terms "the antebellum Black American liberal tradition"[33]—as an antidote to the ideology of racial feudalism that risked preventing "the nation from achieving a civic arrangement that could both preserve liberalism's transformative egalitarian possibilities and enable its widespread practical implementation in ways that did not necessarily depend on group subordination or exclusion."[34] His book restores prominence to names such as William Wells Brown, Frances Ellen Watkins Harper, and Harriet Jacobs, who forged this tradition by seeking to "revise American liberalism by pointing to the praiseworthiness of its aims over the tragedy of its implementation."[35]

I align myself with scholars such as Jacob, Parekh, and Roy, whose historical correctives have shown that women and people of color were not incidental but key to Enlightenment developments and the pursuit of reason in the service of greater freedom, and I argue that reclaiming—or better, *redistributing*—reason is a project that is urgent for our moment. To address the issue of anachronism, I turn to James Schmidt's article on the ways in which the notion of "Enlightenment Project" has become a phantasm of the past onto which those in the present project their concerns. Schmidt argues that "in an effort to draw rhetorically compelling connections between the dreams of the Enlightenment and the nightmares of the twentieth century, otherwise intelligent scholars have wound up making claims about the Enlightenment that border on nonsense."[36] "Nonsense" may be putting it bluntly, but it has become a rhetorical commonplace to assume, pace the early Foucault of *History of Madness*, that the Enlightenment *ideal* of reason is always already an oppressive tool rather than a potentiating one, or that the moral failings of some of the individual human characters best associated with the Enlightenment should cast doubt on the probity of its broader ideas and their potential.

The Motor of the Affective Turn

In the context of the academic humanities, the "affective turn" describes an intellectual trend, arising in the mid-1990s, which focused on the emotions, the body, and experience as previously overlooked valid vectors of academic analysis. It is quite hard to define affect theory precisely since its adherents tend to use a very figurative and impressionistic language to describe it. Editors of *The Affect Theory Reader* (2010), Melissa Greg and Gregory J. Seigworth, for example, title their introduction "An Inventory of Shimmers," and open by announcing "How to begin when, after all, there is no pure or somehow originary state for affect? Affect arises in the midst of *in-between-ness*: in the capacities to act and be acted upon."[37] The closest they come to definition is that "affect" is "synonymous with *force* or *forces of encounter*,"[38] but also something that "transpires within and across the subtlest of shuttling intensities."[39] Moreover it is "potential: a body's *capacity* to affect and be affected."[40] Finally they state—perhaps unsurprisingly: "There is no single, generalizable theory of affect."[41] In the foreword to another volume of essays, *The Affective Turn* (2007), collected together by Patricia Clough based on a series of working groups and seminars she led at City University New York between 1999 and 2006, Michael Hardt claims that "affects refer equally to the mind and body [and] involve both reasons and passion,"[42] yet there is no question but that "reason" and "mind" are the subordinated terms in affect theory. And in her introduction, Clough states that "Affect constitutes a non-linear complexity out of which the narration of conscious states . . . are subtracted," possibly positing affect as the a priori primordial realm from which all thought and feeling are presumed to issue.[43]

Affect theory may have gained the strongest toehold in the fields of queer theory and feminist studies thanks to the influence of Eve Kosofsky Sedgwick's work in the 1990s, which will be the focus of chapter 1. It has also dominated the study of film and visual cultures in recent years and, in fact, has spread across the theoretical humanities to become a ubiquitous methodological norm, even as it remains so ill-defined. It has been most strongly influenced by the branch of philosophy known as phenomenology, which centers the ontology of experience, though the uses to which phenomenological ideas and concepts are put often differ from the context and intentions of their originating texts. The affective turn is a response to a perceived imbalance toward the cerebral, to the detriment of the emotional and the corporeal. It was designed as a reaction against the reification and over-valorization of reason in philosophical traditions that are often marked as "white, masculine," as per my discussion of Enlightenment above. It is, then, perhaps ironic that a turn supposed to speak to those subjects excluded and marginalized from the remit of reason by the likes of Kant (women, queer people, people of color) has as its most influential inspirations authors such as Baruch Spinoza, Sylvan S. Tomkins, Maurice Merleau-Ponty, Gilles Deleuze, and Félix Guattari—all of them white European men. Moreover the lexical and logical complexity of the most densely expressed affective writing owes much to the stylistic tendencies of the last two names.

Differences are noted between "affect," "emotion," and "feelings" in affect theory. In the words of Steven Shaviro, "If emotions are personal experiences, then affects are the forces (perhaps the flows of energy) that precede, produce, and inform such experiences."[44] Affect, then, is something other than a collection of emotions or the field of emotion; Shaviro goes on: "It is social, or even ontological, before it is strictly individual. Affect isn't what I feel, so much as it is what *forces me* to feel."[45] We might take from this, then, that affect is understood as what *propels* feeling—it is emotion's motor or the force behind it. We can see how this definition of "affect" can map onto concepts in various thought systems. For psychoanalysts, the flows of energy subtending and preceding emotions would be Freudian *Triebe* or "drives." For cognitive scientists, affect is a set of preconscious computational processes. For Spinoza, it describes the way in which things in the world *affect* each other. (The verb form is key here; so, affect is a *doing*, not a fixed *thing*.) As already stated, I am looking at affect in this book largely through a Foucault-tinted lens, and I would tentatively argue that, in Foucauldian terms, the flows of energy that are "affect"—understood according to a *discursive* rather than a psychological or neurological framework—might translate to a subtle and multidirectional *pressure to feel* as the "right" way to be affected by the world in our current epoch. The episteme of affect is one in which we are subtly coerced, via a plethora of cultural influences, to prioritize feeling. I add here my own, Foucault-inspired interpretation of how I perceive affect to work, and its status relative to individual feelings and emotions, in order to demonstrate how I understand the field of "affect" that is the target of my critique in this book, and also to suggest that the notion of affect as a "forcefield" has peculiarly Foucauldian resonances that are hitherto unexplored.

I should note that I am not the first writer to think of affect as a *discursive* structure, though affect theory is not often explicitly discussed in these terms. Eric Shouse writes in an article of 2005 that the power of the media lies "not so much in their ideological effects, but in their *ability to create affective resonances* independent of the content or meaning."[46] This is a related argument to the one I am proposing, as it supposes that the stimulation of certain feelings via media and political messaging is separate from a strategy that demands and incentivizes highly emotional reactions as the appropriate ones. I will be arguing throughout this book that the manipulative incitement to feel or the stimulation of strong affective response is the key *mechanism* of contemporary cultural and political rhetoric. Or in other words, certain forms of communication may prime us toward hyperaffective responses, and certain cultural conditions may potentiate or demand this mechanism.

In *The Cultural Politics of Emotion* (2004), Sara Ahmed evaluates and interrogates appeals to emotion in media and political discourse in ways that are resonant with my project. She states: "Rather than asking 'What are emotions?,' I will ask, 'What do emotions do?.'"[47] Yet, unlike my book, Ahmed's work is written from a pro-phenomenological queer perspective; one of her aims is to explore what she calls "the *messiness of the experiential*, how bodies unfold into worlds, and the *drama of contingency*, how we are touched by what comes near."[48] Rather than offering a critique of the deployment of the lexical field of affect as a tool of normative power, then, Ahmed aims to do affect theory better, "beyond thinking of emotion as rhetorical instruments."[49] She wishes to engage its queer promise that she sees as being elsewhere undermined, rather than to question its effectiveness or ethical value tout court.

Another work that is both a contribution to affect theory and a critique of some of its tenets is the book I borrow from in the epigraph of this introduction: Eugenie Brinkema's tour de force *The Forms of the Affects* (2014). Herein, Brinkema, working within the discipline of film studies—one of the disciplines most heavily invested in affect theory—argues that the turn away from close reading or the study of form toward haptics, phenomenology, and audience response has had the negative effect of voiding film scholarship of "detail," "specificity," and "the local." She calls for a "return to reading for form" not as a turn against affect, but in order "to keep its wonderments in revolution, to keep going."[50]

The readings in this book acknowledge and are indebted to a number of scholars who have made critiques of affect in contexts that are parallel to mine, but with different emphases. Probably the most prominent critic of the affective turn in the humanities is Ruth Leys. Her 2011 article, "The Turn to Affect: A Critique," argued that affect theorists in the humanities tend to misunderstand the neuroscience on whose arguments they draw, or to use it partially, or to misrepresent it for their own ends. In 2017, she published her major and weighty tome, *The Ascent of Affect: Genealogy and Critique*. This book meticulously traces the inconsistencies in the understanding of "emotion" and "affect" across both scientific and humanities fields. She shows, via a careful genealogy, the displacement of critique in favor of affect by theorists such as the Deleuze-and-Spinoza-influenced Brian Massumi. In Massumi's work, according to Leys, "attention to ideology or belief is replaced by a focus on bodily affects that are understood to be the outcome of subliminal, autonomic corporeal processes."[51] And, for William Connolly, "what matters politically is how something makes us feel, not what it means to us."[52] Hence, Leys points to the ways in which *content* is often evacuated from affect-theoretical projects, leaving a void of meaning within the structure of the affective forcefield. Leys also notes that while affect theorists claim staunchly anti-Cartesian positions, the essence of their logic consistently separates reason from bodily processes—but valorizes the latter: "Stressing bodies over ideas, affect over reason, the new affect theorists claim that what is crucial is not your beliefs and intentions but the affective processes that are said to produce them, with the result that political change becomes a matter not of persuading others of the truth of your ideas but of producing new ontologies or 'becomings,' new bodies, and new lives."[53] Without stating explicitly that this is her position, Leys appears to oppose the depoliticization of discourse and meaning in the work of many affect theorists, a sentiment with which I am obviously profoundly in agreement and which constitutes one of the explicit aims of this work.

Yet other scholars have written perspicacious critical genealogies of the affective turn that chart the turn's imbrication with specific political moments and their ideologies. In this vein I am thinking especially of Dierdra Reber's argument in *Coming to Our Senses* (2016) that the affective turn marked the point of rupture between "imperial reason" and "neoliberal affect" in the United States and Latin America in the twentieth century,[54] and of Patricia Stuelke's *The Ruse of Repair* (2021), to which I will return in chapter 1, which argues that the affective turn has resulted in "mistaken equations of reparative feeling with collective liberation."[55] She argues here for revisiting the rejection of "critique," pace Rita Felski's much celebrated work of 2015,[56] in a historical perspective, to show how the turn away from what Paul Ricœur called the "hermeneutics of suspicion" may have unintentionally reinforced forms of neoliberal governance in everyday thinking. She asks: "How has anti-imperialism become associated with feeling-as-practice and the rejection of historicism and ideology critique?"[57] Both Reber's and Stuelke's works are focused specifically on the influence of the U.S. context, and especially on the coincidence of a turn to feeling and instances of U.S. administrative and bureaucratic violence, counterinsurgency, and military intervention at different moments in the twentieth century. By contrast, I am writing from the perspective of a European academic, based in the UK, with a continental philosophical bent and a specialism in European cultures. I will, in places, reflect on what the United States has culturally bequeathed to the rest of the Western world by dint of its considerable global influence, but my study will not pursue the United States–centrism or origin claims visible in much of the scholarship in the field.

The most recent work with a parallel agenda with which I will engage is Anna Kornbluh's *Immediacy, or the Style of Too Late Capitalism* (2024), an ambitious attempt to counter the ubiquitous fashion for what Kornbluh calls "immediacy" in criticism, culture, and artistic production with a return to "mediation." Immediacy, as she describes it, adumbrates the affective turn insofar as it "mires itself in profundities of corporeality, affect, and polarized extremity"[58] and promotes "phenomenology as [the] limit horizon for knowledge."[59] With chapters covering autotheory and autofictions, including misery memoirs, selfies, and video streaming, the book argues that self-indulgent, overly personalized, present-centered, and trauma-soaked production both emblematizes our stylistic zeitgeist and passes as a virtue. To this perceived scourge of immediacy, Kornbluh proposes "mediation"—which is similar to how critical theory used to look before it took an immediate/affective detour. "Conceptually," she writes, "the project of critical theory has been to work through symptoms and resistances, to propel thought through impasses, to negate what is merely given, and then to negate the negation, convoking readers to collective composition."[60] What we now have instead is academics "opting to drown in the extremity of bad affects without the punctuating relation to an other."[61]

While I find Kornbluh's observations imaginatively generative, and will return to her ideas in chapter 4 and the conclusion, I depart from the author's position in several ways. First, I do not deprecate the idea of the individual or "self" and unquestioningly laud the collective as a panacea to the ills of the present. This is partly because I do not think, as was the argument of my earlier book, *Selfish Women*, that rational selfhood has yet been historically acknowledged as proper to all subjects.[62] I see no evidence of communism having delivered human flourishing, and I look instead to liberal, secular models that uphold cooperative individuality as an ideal for better thinking and being. Secondly, and relatedly, I do not think that what Kornbluh calls "mediation" and I call "redistributive reason" requires radical depersonalization. Kornbluh has much to say about first- and third-person narratives in fiction, with the turn in popularity toward the former and away from the latter marking the characteristic of immediacy she calls "personalism." Indeed, Kornbluh's book is written without the author ever making an "I" statement and, in the conclusion, it is written: "In quest of that other style, this mediation against immediacy, this book synthesizes at saucy scale, speaks impersonally without "I," and composes prose that holds off intuition and holds out interpretation."[63] Ironically, perhaps, this statement conveys just as nicely a sense of the author's individual intention and attitude as if she had simply written "I." One can, without fetishizing the neoliberal subject, or in Kornbluh's words the "individuated 'I' complex of the private contemporary,"[64] and without asssuming personal, so-called lived experience to be the only form of access to truth, acknowledge one's subjectivity and write from it while still respecting and welcoming the horizon of a more objective critical and political mode than is the current fashion. That will be my technique in what follows.

The Contents of this Book

In chapter 1, I evaluate the affective turn in queer theory as paradigmatic of the academic shift over the past thirty years from analysis to affect; from critique to repair. I discuss how Eve Kosofsky Sedgwick's call for a move from a position of "paranoia" (the hermeneutics of suspicion) to a position of "reparation" (a "positive" affective approach to objects) has had effects that have reached into, and way beyond, queer studies, the humanities, and the bounds of the academy itself to influence broader cultural norms.

Chapter 2 explores the discursive currency of empathy, which I term an "emotion on speed," since it describes the ability not only to feel acutely, but also to feel other people's feelings. Empathy is widely assumed, both in much therapeutic discourse and in everyday cultural parlance, to be an unalloyed moral good. I first discuss the ideas of a number of pro-empathy exponents, before exploring rational ethical models that have been offered as alternatives to empathy, especially those proposed by psychologist Paul Bloom. I consider why these alternatives are not more widely valorized, concluding that it is precisely empathy's over-saturation with feeling that makes it currently so highly rated in our hyperaffective age.

Chapter 3 discusses the stakes of hurt feelings and the language of offense-as-harm that are central elements of what has been dubbed a "culture war" over the past decade or so. This is often traced to the emergence of a censorious left-wing ideological culture that has taken root within Anglophone universities. Critiques of this phenomenon tend to focus on how contemporary leftist discourse promulgates the belief that causing another to feel offense is a form of "literal violence" and argue that, on the basis of such claims, the left deploys tools of censorship to close down the possibility of offense-giving. My chapter attempts to restore balance to this highly charged debate by also assessing the equally emotive deployment of rhetoric from the cultural right wing.

I examine in detail the arguments of some of the most high-profile critics of "woke culture" including the Canadian psychologist Jordan Peterson, whose writing I read in tandem with Judith Butler's *Who's Afraid of Gender?* (2024) to show

how similar emotive rhetorical strategies are used by those on "both sides." Where the left explicitly prioritizes "the vulnerable," the right pushes for a patrician resilience that embodies regressive stereotypes about traditional values and plays on nostalgic impulses, while also borrowing the label of "victim," albeit for the white male subject whose historical dominance is perceived to be under threat. This shared ideology, amply deployed by both left and right, has given rise to what I term "the Tyranny of Vulnerability." I argue that, on all points of the political compass, emotive critique is being prioritized over reasoned debate—ironically, perhaps *especially* by those wielding a putative right-wing "common-sense" form of "reason" as their mode of attack on the excesses of the left.

Chapter 4 takes the cultural temperature of the COVID-19 pandemic. It undertakes to re-read the concept of "vulnerability," discussed as a weaponized discourse in chapter 3, as a placemarker for imagining the redistribution of reason to subjects outside of the unmarked, healthy population in the context of a public health crisis. It further undertakes an analysis of some of the ways that the pandemic was written as an intrinsically emotionally overburdened phenomenon, as per Anna Kornbluh's concept of "immediacy," by the manipulative government, media, and public health machinery and by cultural commentators attempting to make sense of it alike. Reading "plague texts" by Judith Butler, Laura Dodsworth, and Jacqueline Rose, I submit that a more rational and less emotive response could have had the beneficent effect of producing less "dis-ease" in an age of disease.

I conclude the book by arguing that the turn to feeling across a number of spheres in recent decades has not led to a feminist or progressive utopia—in fact, quite the reverse. The popularity and creep of affect theory from the academy to the public sphere has had the dual effect of reversing the value judgments ascribed to reason and feeling, while continuing to align feeling and the body with non-male, non-normative subjects, in a way that is strikingly—if unintentionally—reactionary. In closing, I turn to Audre Lorde's 1977 essay "Poetry is Not a Luxury" and read surprising resonances between it and Foucault's 1984 essay on the Enlightenment to argue that together they may offer the blueprint for a path toward a third way that I call a "Feminist Neo-Enlightenment"—the state proper to redistributed reason. I then sketch some ways in which this may look different from other, recent calls for rationality, for example that propounded by Steven Pinker in his *Enlightenment Now* (2018).

Drawing together the findings of the book, I argue for tempering the fashion for emotional outpouring with a renewed commitment to analytical critique. I call for a reinstatement of the values of freedom of expression (however hurtful some expression may be) and reason as an ideal (if not always a perfectly executable one—since the perfect should not be the enemy of the good) as the most likely pathways to the fullest potential of both liberty for the self and compassion and respect for others. I urge progressives to stand behind these values and to reject the Tyranny of Vulnerability in an age of ever-proliferating disinformation, manipulation, and uncertainty.

1
Repairing What Wasn't Broken

Queer Theory's Affective Turn

Foucault became synonymous with paranoid reading: to be paranoid was to be Foucauldian.
—Lynne Huffer, "Foucault and Queer Theory"

Here, in a present in which the value of critical thinking has undergone attrition in contemporary cultures that prioritise accounting without accountability, discourse without truth, and meaning without interpretation, the reparative turn quite significantly rewrites the critic's value as the consequence of the object's need.
—Robyn Wiegman, "The Times We're In: Queer Feminist Criticism and the Reparative 'Turn'"

My methodological commitment in this book is to understanding the workings of the academic and cultural affective turns by borrowing implements from Foucault's tool kit, where useful, and combining them with a feminist ethic. This methodological choice is, in part, a deliberate gesture against the way queer theory, the branch of the theoretical humanities perhaps most indebted to and influenced by Foucault since its first days, has progressively embraced the affective turn and rejected Foucault. In so doing, queer theory has turned its back on the critical-analytical methods (dubbed "paranoid") that Foucault and his poststructuralist peers offered, and with which his name became synonymous, as per Huffer's words in the first quotation of this chapter's epigraph.

Queer was a politics and a praxis before it was a theory. In the 1980s, the decade of Foucault's death from an HIV-related illness, grassroots activists under the banners of ACT UP and Queer Nation formed strategic alliances in order to protest against homophobia, racism, and the hatred faced by recreational drug users, uniting the targets of HIV moral panic. David Halperin has argued that the work of ACT UP marked a genuinely Foucauldian act of resistance to authority via strategies of resignification and defiant mockery rather than revolutionary momentum.[1] And, crucially, these movements took the hateful slur "queer" and, in a gesture of reverse-discourse, recuperated it not as an *identity* but as a *positionality*, bringing together and giving voice to those marginalized by the mainstream with a common cause. Once embedded in the academy, the theoretical-methodological underpinnings of "queer" involved a rough methodological division between a Foucauldian approach, focused on the workings of antinormative critique, of reverse-discursive practice, and of power analysis, and a psychoanalytical (usually Lacanian) one, drawing attention to the fundamentally unfixed, unstable, chaotic nature of desire in order to queer utilitarian or hegemonic meanings of (hetero)sexuality.[2] The Foucauldian-inspired mode of queer theory in particular came under fire with the turn to affect in queer associated with Eve Kosofsky Sedgwick's introduction of the notion of "the reparative." This turn has psychoanalytical underpinnings, but borrows from Melanie Klein's object relations theory rather than Lacan's more anarchic theory of desire, rendering more recent forays in queer, as Oliver Davis and Tim Dean have recently pointed out,[3] somewhat devoid of a concern with sex.

When one thinks of Sedgwick's work on affect, it is her collection *Touching Feeling* (2003), which brings together Melanie Klein and Sylvan Tompkins with Buddha and Proust, that immediately comes to mind, locating queer's affective turn in the early 2000s. However, Robyn Wiegman and Lynne Huffer have both pointed out that Sedgwick's interest in affect goes all the way back to her first writings on related subjects in the late 1980s and early 1990s.[4] The key piece of writing articulating the terms of Sedgwick's affective shift that is included in *Touching Feeling* under the admittedly excellent title, "Paranoid Reading and Reparative Reading; or You're So Paranoid, You Probably Think This Essay Is about You," is a reworking of a piece first published in 1996 and expanded for republication in 1997. Sedgwick's work in this mode suggests a reorientation of queer's objectives away from a unique focus on the hermeneutics of suspicion (or the "paranoid position" in Kleinian terms)—toward a so-called reparative position. She uses Kleinian psychoanalysis and Tompkins's work on affect to flesh out these terms. Sedgwick argues that the suspicious or paranoid position had become "nearly synonymous with criticism itself,"[5] closing down the possibility of other modes of response or other "positions." Her argument here is nuanced and careful. She does not argue that the reparative should *entirely* eclipse the paranoid, or that we should excessively (re)pathologize paranoia, but rather she is interested in foregrounding "the powerful reparative practices that . . . infuse self-avowedly paranoid critical projects."[6] And she states: "It seems to me a great loss when paranoid inquiry comes to seem entirely coextensive with critical theoretical inquiry rather than being viewed as one kind of cognitive/affective theoretical practice among other, alternative kinds."[7]

Her claim is that, in an age in which state abuses of power are so egregious and so obvious, a strategy of identifying, interpreting, and analyzing the workings of power in, for example, a Foucauldian vein, may be redundant. She situates this claim by recounting her discussion with an activist friend, Cindy Patton, about the hypothesized origins of HIV: Was it developed in a lab by the U.S. military? Was it intended as a bioweapon to target gay men, drug users, and African populations? Sedgwick reflects on Patton's refusal to speculate on the grounds that, even if its origins were uncovered: "What would we know then that we don't already know?"[8] That some lives and bodies are valued over others by the governing classes is not something that needs revealing, Sedgwick notes. She goes on to state that knowing the origin story of HIV would not fundamentally *change* anything, but that that drive to uncover knowledge is deeply ingrained and tells us something about then-contemporary (paranoid) modes of thinking. Sedgwick asks us to consider an approach to objects that is less cynical, less circumscribing, and more open-ended than the paranoid method. A flavor of what this might look like is found in Klein's description of the reparative approach to depression in which the subject adopts "a guilty, empathetic view of the other as at once good, damaged, integral, and requiring and eliciting love and care."[9] Yet, while only suggesting here a provisional strategy of approaching objects from a different position, the totalizing impact of Sedgwick's legacy, both within and beyond queer theory, can, to my mind, not be exaggerated. Indeed, I would go so far as to state that some of the problems I identify in this book are encapsulated in the above-cited formulation. For example in the next chapter I undertake a critique of the presumed benefit of holding an "empathic view of the other," in a culture in which empathy has become unquestioningly synonymous with ethics, while in chapter 3 I turn to the cultural phenomenon of weaponized vulnerability, by means of which intersubjective relations have become dependent upon on a "guilty" fetishization and deployment of the privilege-vulnerability couple as the entire mode of social life on the left. These ideas that Sedgwick floats here, as alternatives to a perceived sclerotic norm, have become concretized as imperatives in the current day.

It was not inevitable that a creeping, joyless spirit of affective compulsion should have been the outcome, and I do not think that this was what Sedgwick intended. Indeed, she states that her proposed turn away from the suspicious mode is partly in the service of inviting "surprise," aesthetic and sensory engagement, and "hope" into the encounters between critics and objects—rejuvenating them with a playfulness and openness.[10] The gesture of taking the object on its own terms rather than seeking to interpret it laid some groundwork for the imaginative and paradigm-shifting new materialist writing of theorists such as Karen Barad that seeks to evacuate individual human agency and intentionality from the encounters between objects. However it also inspired a glut of affective work that addresses political and cultural problems from the standpoint of emotional engagement. Indeed, in an essay from 2014 describing the then-current state of what she calls "queer feminist criticism," Robyn Wiegman identifies "affect" and "temporality" as the defining themes or features of queer feminist work in the 2000s and 2010s and attributes the spread of them to the influence of Sedgwick's interventions.[11] Wiegman enumerates prominent recent publications that contribute to this density of focus on affect, citing Ann Cvetkovich on trauma as a response to capitalism, Lauren Berlant's notion of repetitive living as slow death, Elizabeth Povinelli on the affective dimensions of subjugation, Sharon Holland on racism's affectively dense erotic life, Sara Ahmed's call for rage and hope as a counter to the promise of happiness, and disorientation and disidentification as utopian gestures in works by José Esteban Muñoz and Jack Halberstam.[12]

All of these works focus on forms of feeling (individual or collective) rather than on critique as the appropriate response to social injustice and culture's ills.

The tendency of this move(ment) is, arguably, an—unintended—neoliberalizing one, as it describes a shift away from the analysis and critique of the conditions creating injustice or oppression toward a focus on self-expression and self-care as reparative tools—a move from looking outward to looking inward. Indeed, in her book *The Ruse of Repair* that I discussed briefly in my introduction, Stuelke argues that the reparative turn, which she calls "this glide that so often is articulated as a relief from the exhaustion of struggling against structural violence that never seems to abate or recede,"[13] has, in fact, resulted in "mistaken equations of reparative feeling with collective liberation."[14] There is perhaps an ironic truth in this creeping neoliberalization of queer thought itself, since Wiegman understands the reparative turn in the context of "scholars negotiating university environments increasingly engulfed in the insecurity and ambivalence of neoliberalisation."[15] In this context she claims that reparative criticism is "a compensatory tactic aimed at redeeming the critic's self-perception in the twilight of the hermeneutics of suspicion, where one of the most potent remnants of its critical habits can be found in the repeated accusation that the declining significance of the humanities is the critic's own fault."[16] Hence the reparative turn appears here to be a gesture of defeat that may unwittingly repeat the logic of the system that holds academics in its thrall and demoralizes them.

Indeed Wiegman's own position on the reparative turn in her 2014 article is quite hard to pin down, as it appears to me to be characterized by ambivalence. In a memorable passage of her article that I use as the second epigraph of this chapter, so central to our concerns does it seem to me, she describes the zeitgeist (in 2014) as one in which values are in flux, a present in which "the value of critical thinking has undergone attrition" such that we are accustomed to witnessing "accounting without accountability, discourse without truth, and meaning without interpretation."[17] It is in this context that she understands the impulse for Sedgwick's reparative turn—against making ever more interpretations of an ever emptier world and instead toward forms of aesthetic, sensory, and emotional appreciation. If we provisionally grant Sedgwick and those "pro-affectives" who come in her wake the validity of the claim that, in an age in which state exercise of discrimination and violence is explicit, it is redundant to ask how or why, or cui bono?, then we might want to check—almost thirty years later than Sedgwick's musings and a decade after Wiegman's summary of their influence—whether that characterization of the zeitgeist still holds firm. In 2025, the terms "misinformation" and "disinformation" circulate widely, almost as much as dubious information itself, in a social media–saturated age in which TikTok passes for a news channel and presidents, premiers, and politicians of all stripes test the popularity of policies on Elon Musk's X (the platform formerly known as "Twitter"). While such a culture drips with conspiracy theories, a hermeneutics of suspicion that attempts not only to discern truth from lies but to analyze the motivations of these, can surely no longer easily be dismissed as passé or seen as anything other than necessary and *reasonable*, and calling suspicion "paranoid" in this context seems off-color. It is perhaps precisely from my location in 2025, then, in the wake of Trump (x2), Brexit, COVID-19, Russia's assault on Ukraine, and renewed violence in the Middle East, that I find the gesture of approaching the world firstly via affective attachments and reparative self-care, and only secondarily via reasoned political critique, less than compelling.

Sedgwick suggests that suspicious critique—as "paranoid"—is

itself always already a form of affect, not (just) a form of reasoning. She suggests that paranoia has been a particularly tempting mechanism for queer theory to rest on because of the association in Freudian thought between homosexuality and paranoia: The theory apes the object. Analogously, she points out the example of Freud recognizing that his own psychoanalytic method was paranoid in relation to the Schreber case, aligning him and his method irresistibly with his analysand. Sedgwick characterizes the paranoid position, after Silvan Tomkins's formulation, as a "strong" affect theory, specifically a "strong negative affect theory,"[18] to which the reparative position as "weak" and "positive" is counterposed. The very choice to label the form of critique she writes against as "paranoid" is telling in more than one way. First, we might note that naming a critical trend "paranoid"—*diagnosing* it with a label from the psy sciences—is itself a somewhat paranoid, rather than reparative, thing to do. This suggests that every bit as much as the critic nominally in search of reason and truth will also, inevitably, be influenced by (disavowed) emotion—as the affect theorists wish us to recognize—so too does the project of identifying "better" modes of critical response (affect) involve an interpretative cognitive process, even if the object it settles on is affect. The impossibility of a "total eclipse" works both ways.

Wither Reason? Wither Norms?

Although the establishment of the opposing pair reparative-paranoid, with the valuing of the former over the latter, marks a particularly intensive affective moment in queer theory's history, the slippery but generative term "reason" has long been absent from queer's tool kit, in line with the suspicion of rationality that is central to the thought of Foucault (though his relationship to it is ambivalent and shifting, as previously noted) and the other figures of Critical Theory that underpin queer. Indeed, going further than most thinkers of the 1970s and 1980s who shaped it, queer has imagined itself resolutely in opposition to the ideal of reason.

This can be seen in less theoretically dense and more, one might say, pragmatic or applied works of queer theory, as well as in the formative theoretical texts that establish the wobbly canon of queer. For example, in their fine 2010 book on queer and research methodology, focusing especially on how queer can in any meaningful way be brought to bear on, combined with, or made to transform more traditional social sciences methodologies, editors Kath Browne and Catherine Nash and their contributors return repeatedly to the problem of reason. In the editors' introduction, Browne and Nash comment on the way in which poststructuralism and postmodernism—movements that birthed queer—moved from reifying to dethroning, and then to deconstructing, the unmarked subject of reason (the white, straight, cis, middle-class, etcetera man): "Work in the humanities challenges the conceptualisation of the modern Enlightenment subject as rational, unified and stable. Within postmodernist theorising, broadly conceptualised, scholars took critical aim at claims about a universal human condition and the linear tale of a progressive human history as artificial, improbable and unduly homogenising of the human experience."[19] It is undeniable that the construct of the universal "homogenizing" human subject has historically been a narrow and exclusionary one—a white, moneyed man. But, as I discussed in the introduction, it is as troubling as it is incorrect to suggest that the nature of subordinate subjects should remain defined by the terms of their oppressor. The recuperation of so-called feminine virtues—emotion, care and embodiedness—for queer and feminist work is an *understandable* counterstrategy to the lauding of masculine rationality, but not, I am arguing, the best one. The qualities known as "reason" are in no meaningful, tangible, or transcendent way "masculine." Reason can belong to everyone and to no one. I argue that a more effective strategy is not to challenge the *quality* of reason but to expand the remit of the kind of person and subjective positionality that may be deemed capable of that ideal quality. In this book, I term this strategy *redistributing reason*.

The ways in which resistance to reason is articulated in queer are perfectly illustrated in a formulation in the chapter of Brown and Nash's book coauthored by Andrew Gorman-Murray, Linda Johnston, and Gordon Waitt. They write of themselves, as queer scholars: "We are committed to complex and critical understandings of reflexivity and self, opening up explorations of non-rational, non-(hetero)normative and noncolonial dimensions of research relationships."[20] The equivalence suggested here between "rationality," "heteronormativity," and "colonialism" as "bad objects" prompts me to ask whether the former term really is the same *category* of object as the latter two. Heteronormativity and colonialism are instances of structural forms of oppression, with a specific content, in which given groups and systems oppress or demonstrate bias toward particular, subaltern populations or marginalized groups. Reason—unlike the other two concepts, to which a dynamic of oppression and subordination is *intrinsic*—is arguably problematic only insofar as it has historically been assumed to be properly the possession or character of a powerful subject, as I have discussed, and thereby implicated in the racist and sexist logics of that subject. Yet reason—characterized, for example, by rigorous critical thinking and by the scientific method which is arguably, at base, one of the most democratic of methods because, by definition, it is reproducible anywhere by anyone—is a quality that is largely intrinsically beneficent to all. (The horrific abuses of eugenics do *not* constitute a sound argument against the *principle* of the scientific method.) It is almost as if the ideal of reason is not being rejected because it is impossible to carry out perfectly, but because it has become *intrinsically* tainted or suspect *qua* idea, via its historical ascription to the domain of the heteromasculine, in a way that almost appears superstitious—and very irrational.

In volume 1 of his *History of Sexuality, The Will to Knowledge* (first published in France in 1976), Foucault famously carries out a master class in reverse-discursive thinking by showing that, in giving names to sexual personages—"the invert," "the pervert"—the sexologists of the nineteenth century succeeded not only in pathologizing them, but in creating the conditions for forms of resistant pleasure-and-community-making on the basis of shared subjectivization. Similarly, although it is used to designate that which the sovereign subject possessed, "reason" is just as available for discursive and strategic about-turns, for being used against the grain. I would argue that if the ideal of reason were not the better, more productive, more pleasurable virtue, the eighteenth-century Enlightened patriarch would not have claimed it for himself as the proper condition of maleness and attributed to women, people of color, and other nonnormative subjects, emotion or unreason. The continued lauding of the nonrational or the antirational in theory simply means that reason—a limitless intellectual resource—is not adequately shared. And we might ask why, unlike other objects ripe for reverse-discursive treatment (such as the pathologizing sexual labels at the very foundation of "queer's" coming-into-being as a grass roots response to the homophobia of the AIDS crisis), reason remains largely off-limits as recuperable.

The queer affective turn's rejection of "paranoid critique" foreshadows a tendency in some more recent writing to question a central concept bequeathed by Foucault to queer theory: antinormativity. In her much-praised *The Limits of Critique*, published in 2015, Rita Felski takes aim at "an antinormative normativity" that she sees as intrinsic to the suspicious project of "critique" tout court.[21] And, also in 2015, a special issue of the journal *differences* edited by Wiegman and Elizabeth Wilson devoted itself to "Queer Theory without Antinormativity"[22] in order to ask what queer theory might become were it not wedded to a project of opposition to "the norm," its "axiomatic foe."[23] In their introduction, the editors assert that "a defense against normativity is a guiding tenet of queer inquiry, as central to its self-definition as the anti-identitarianism that enabled the famed departure of *queer* from the rubrics of *lesbian* and *gay*."[24] They go on to claim that the emphasis on norm-opposition has led to a myopic focus of inquiry that occludes other possible queer approaches and projects, and blocks scholars from "channel[ing] the energies of queer inquiry otherwise"[25]—though what this "otherwise" might look like remains undefined.

Several of the contributions to the special issue focus on alleged misunderstandings or overdeterminations of "normativity" and its antithesis that muddy the waters of queer. In their introduction, the editors write: "Even as it allies itself with Foucault, queer theory has maintained an attachment to the politics of oppositionality (against, against, against) that form the infrastructure of the repressive hypothesis,"[26] and in her article, Annamarie Jagose writes that the meaning of the term "antinormativity" has been unstable throughout queer theory's corpus such that it functions only as queer's "field-founding force"[27] and "as queer theory's privileged figure for the political."[28] These assertions rest largely on Jagose's reading of Judith Butler's foundational text *Gender Trouble* (1990) in which, she claims, Butler uses "normative" in ways that are not strictly Foucauldian. While this may be a fair assessment of Butler, I am not convinced that it offers a compelling rationale for abandoning a critical project of queer antinormativity going forward.

Normativity is a very rich concept. In the context of this book project, I want to think briefly about its affective properties.

Prizing the norm suggests an affective attachment to tradition, to convention, to straightness, to mediocrity, to not deviating, to the same, to the status quo—but also to the latest fashion or fad, to group think, to majoritarianism, and to thinking with not against. The *content* of the norm is not fixed, but a conservative or conformist cleaving-to characterizes its forms. Antinormative impulses are ones that pull against and ask us to think differently, that reveal problems of logic or bias in the norm—be it a longstanding norm or the latest fad that is passing as the unimpeachable epitome of progress—and that shine light on wrinkles in what is apparently ordinary, unmarked, or natural. In a review of the 2015 special issue posted on the blog "Bully Bloggers," Jack Halberstam writes wittily that the only answer provided to the editors' central question "What is queer studies without antinormativity?" is "It is disciplinary, neoliberal, no stakes, straight thinking. You're welcome!"[29] I share Halberstam's reservations about a project of anti-antinormative queer theory that disavows the need for questioning, probing, nuanced opposition and that strives to "disarticulate" queer "from radicality."[30] Moreover, I would suggest that a method of *antinormative redistributive reason* is a recuperative strategy that queer theory would do well to tarry with in the current hyperaffective climate in which the episteme of affect *is* the new normativity.

Some Concluding Remarks

It is irresistible, if cynical (but, as should by now be clear, I am very much not ready to relinquish cynicism), to suspect that one thing that may be going on in the arcane reaches of the most theoretical branches of the humanities is a search for novelty that is reckless in its casting off of methods and concepts formerly valorized by that cluster of disciplines. The wholesale rejection of values that might be considered "traditional," "hegemonic," or "establishment," such as the much-maligned "reason," is understandable for a body of theory such as queer—albeit, I have argued, a tactical mistake. But I am also interested here in what *from within queer* is currently being cast aside. It is at the level of *internal* critique that the rejection of strategies deemed "paranoid" and the key concept of "antinormativity" operates, while the continued rejection of reason is a rejection of an object *external* to it. This, I am arguing, is a dual error, as the former are ripe for revalorization and the latter for redistribution.

There is a constant search in academia in general, and in the theoretical humanities perhaps most of all, for "the new." The phenomenon of a succession of "turns"—the affective/reparative, the antisocial, the ethical, the postsecular, and so on—inevitably means that the fundamental measure of "fashion" becomes deterministic of what is valued. It is in this spirit that, if a theory (for example Foucauldian anti/normativity) has been around for a long time, it may become *intrinsically suspect* because it is not sufficiently fresh (regardless of whether it is still—or as I would argue in this particular case, more than ever—useful and generative). I have made parallel arguments elsewhere regarding the recent dismissal and, indeed, demonization, of earlier forms of feminism (the disputedly termed "second-wave" radical tradition) because of a taint of political impurity or failure to live up to the specific values and methods of twenty-first-century feminism on the part of some third- and fourth-wavers. There is a tendency in current feminism to write about its buzzwords and values as if they are the sole valid markers of ethics and define the transcendent, evolved high point of progress—even as "progress" remains a nominally suspicious object for the present moment, linked as it is to an Enlightenment way of thinking and insufficiently to affect.[31] But does it have to be this way?

In her chapter of my edited book, *After Foucault* (2018), Lynne Huffer offers a fresh and valuable corrective to the assumed split this chapter has described between "critical" queer and "affective" queer. By charting a subtle genealogy of Sedgwick's relation to Foucault from the explicitly pro-Foucault Sedgwick of *Epistemology of the Closet* (1990) to her later contra-Foucault position in her work on Klein, Tompkins, and affect, Huffer suggests that we might view the paranoid-reparative shift slightly differently: not as a moment of violent rupture, but as a move that also contained within it an awareness of the affective power of Foucault's work that has made it so *effective*. Moreover, Huffer argues that while Sedgwick's writing itself is subtle and nuanced, it is the instrumentalizing structure of the academy, the very structure that produces disciplines in the first place, that reifies bodies of theory and constructs distinct "turns" that close off the rich potential of the past from the promise of future scholarship.

I will cite Huffer at length here, as what she writes is of great relevance to my current argument: "The codification of queer theory is not only paradoxical but also constitutive of what is now understood as queer. . . . The same codification has transformed Foucault and Sedgwick into the flat simulacra of their original work. Just as Foucault's mind- altering histories of sexuality became conventionalized as a paranoid queer theory whose only aim was the unveiling of masked violence, so too Sedgwick's explorations of a more reparative queer theory . . . have been generalized and tossed into the academic grab bag of affect theory."[32] I concur with Huffer that this codification or delimitation is indeed what happens in the discipline-bound academy with its imposition of frameworks such as "ruptures" and "turns." I would add that, when the theory slips out of academia and into the public sphere, the nuanced thinking and rich ambiguity within the texture of the writing is even more lost. Sedgwick herself writes that "Everyday theory qualitatively affects everyday knowledge and experience."[33] Here she means, in the context of the 1990s, that the dominance of paranoid theory means that everyone is excessively and unhelpfully cynical, negative, and paranoid. But that same observation may also be applied to the 2020s, with a different resonance, as I would argue that the current dominance of affect theory may mean that everyone is excessively and unhelpfully aware of perceived vulnerability, porously open to feeling, and hypervigilant to offense—as I will explore in chapter 3.

It is my conviction that, if it is to continue to have teeth, the central modus of queer theory—and work in the theoretical humanities more broadly—has to remain that of *thinking about and against*, rather than (or, if you insist, as well as) *feeling*. It has to hold on to the antinormativity that made queer an effective grassroots activist tool in the first place. Crucially, we must remain attentive to what the norm actually *is*, since norms shift. And if the present norm is indeed a glut of idealized feeling, which is the thesis I am prosecuting here, then the only appropriate stance for queer (or any other counterhegemonic discourse) to take would be a strategic, antinormative embrace of "reason" (understood, as per the discussion in the introduction, as a form of pointed critical thinking—of "daring to know" in Kant's words)—however counterintuitive that may appear. The reparative position, at best, implies a stepping back from a relentless, exhausting suspicion of power abuse and conspiracy-theory-tarrying. But, at what cost does this come? At worst, it implies a form of defeatism—that what we cannot control we should not seek to understand or critique. It is *primarily* in its logical conclusion that the so-called strong affect of critique is redundant that, I argue, the actual weakness of the affective turn lies.

2

Why Aren't We Minding Our Own Shoes?

On Empathy

People often assume that empathy is an absolute good.
You can never be too rich or too thin . . . or too empathic.
—Paul Bloom, *Against Empathy*

In the summer of 2023, Greta Gerwig's five-hundred-million-dollar-grossing film *Barbie*, a witty and whimsical tale of a very pink "femocracy," lit up cinema screens across the globe. As a movie tie-in, here in the UK, free Barbie and Ken dolls were given to children in seven hundred schools under the label of Mattel's "Barbie School of Friendship" program. This program was designed to teach "social skills such as empathy" to children via role-play, an aim which the company says was based on neuroscientific research.[1] In a news analysis piece for the *British Medical Journal*, Hristio Boytchev reported that Mattel's program had been criticized for engaging in "stealth marketing."[2] This public relations move suggests that "teaching empathy" is assumed to be such an unquestionable social good that it was deliberately front-loaded as the overt motivation for what is, arguably, a cynical commercial campaign.

This chapter examines the privileging, in some branches of the psy sciences as well as in much everyday discourse, of the rather ill-defined but heavy-lifting concept of "empathy." Empathy, I argue, functions as a sort of superaffective signifier, an emotion on speed, since it describes, loosely, the capacity of *feeling what the other is feeling, as if I were in their shoes*. In his aptly titled *The Age of Empathy*, primatologist Frans de Waal triumphantly claimed in 2009, in the wake of Barack Obama's presidential win, that "greed is out, empathy is in,"[3] setting the two terms in opposition to each other as apparently self-evident signifiers of moral "good" and "bad," while Steven Pinker wrote in 2011 of the twenty-first century as an era characterized by an "empathy craze."[4] The belief that empathy is a synonym for social good, as per the quotation from Paul Bloom in my epigraph, underpins Mattel's pro-empathy rhetorical campaign choice, just one rather egregious example of the broader concepts of "emotional branding"[5] or "empathy marketing"[6] that have become fashionable in the worlds of public relations and advertising.

The capaciousness, slipperiness, and therefore necessary imprecision of empathy as a concept is noted by Amy Coplan in an article of 2011, wherein she claims that empathy "has come to occupy a central role in countless debates taking place in both public and academic discourse."[7] Similarly, Carolyn Pedwell contends that empathy, which she defines as "the ability to put oneself in the other's shoes"[8] is commonly perceived as "the panacea to a wide range of social, political and economic divisions and grievances,"[9] and "what we want to cultivate in ourselves and others."[10] However, I would note that the ability to *feel into* the other's emotional world does not guarantee a response of altruism or care. Indeed some argue, against the commonplace that psychopaths do not feel empathy, that they may in fact have the capacity for huge amounts of cognitive empathy (or theory of mind, that is an awareness of other people's inner worlds), but low levels of emotional empathy, which precisely allows the nefarious among them better to manipulate their victims.[11] What those termed psychopaths may precisely lack, instead, is a capacity for compassion. In what follows, I will sketch the history of empathy, examine some of the positive claims made for it, and then turn to extant critiques of it, and, in keeping with the method and aims of the book, I will show how empathy may be discursively used and abused in ways that are potentially socially and ethically manipulative, in line with the affective episteme in which we live. In short, I will question the value of a concept that, in its purest form, is so rationally limited, and that places such huge emotional expectations on us, that the lionization of it may be unwarranted.

A Brief History of Empathy

The German term *Einfühlung* (translated into English as "empathy") came into use in 1873 with the literal meaning of "feeling into" or "in-feeling." However, the idea behind the process we now call "empathy" has arguably existed since long before the age of modernity. Some evolutionary theorists argue that it may be central to our adaptation as a social species, while historians of emotions locate its efflorescence in the context of the Enlightenment—the historical-cultural moment at which an awareness of the inner life of others became possible. Maria Scott has pointed out in her study of empathy and the modern literary imagination (2020) that the German term was first used by the philosopher Robert Vischer as a specifically *aesthetic* concept, describing a "projection of the self into the object of beauty."[12] This accounts for the literary critical commonplace that reading empathically is an improving good, though Scott likens empathic reading instead to a kind of manipulative seduction. It would then become a predominantly moral concept, with philosophers such as David Hume and Adam Smith identifying the mechanism as the prerequisite for prosocial behavior.

An early pre-echo of the modern notion of "empathy" is the term "sympathy," which has subtly changed meaning over time. In the eighteenth century, sympathy denoted the *feeling into* or *feeling as* that we now describe as empathy, while "sympathy" has come to mean feeling *for* someone, a concept lacking the sense of sharedness or affective integration that "empathy" suggests. Peter Goldie, in *The Emotions*, makes mention of various types of sympathy, citing "pity, commiseration, concern and compassion."[13] Phenomenologist Edmund Husserl defined empathy in *Phänomenologische Psychologie* (1925) as "the intentionality in one's own ego that leads into the foreign ego."[14]

Drawing on the work of Husserl, Swiss German psychiatrist and philosopher Karl Jaspers wrote in his *General Psychopathology* of 1913 that "rational understanding is merely an aid to psychology, empathic understanding brings us to psychology itself."[15] Jaspers's psychiatric method focused on the excavation of hidden, subjective phenomena that patients bring to the clinical encounter, alongside the observable, objective ones. These subjective phenomena are the lived world experience of the patient that the psychiatrist must try to share in. While Jaspers acknowledged the need for the psychiatrist to understand and interpret, he argued that any method that stops there lacks a crucial dimension that is "a matter of pure experience, not of explicit knowledge."[16] This matter of pure experience is accessed, it is claimed, through empathy.

However, the hard limit of the psychiatrist's capacity to experience the patient's inner world, according to Jaspers, is schizophrenic psychosis, which is labelled "unknowable." Schizophrenia is commonly understood to mark the break with intellectual reason as a shared human code. Yet, given that Jaspers had characterized empathy as "spontaneous" and "nonintellectual,"[17] we might wonder why patients with schizophrenia should not also be approached in this way. This perhaps points to a flaw in Jasper's logic, according to which rationality is the *aid* to understanding; empathy the *thing itself*. Despite empathy apparently operating outside of the sphere of the intellectual for Jaspers, schizophrenia is nevertheless seen to lie beyond its reach, suggesting the limitations of Jaspers's conception of empathy—or perhaps the limitations of empathy itself. More recent phenomenological practitioners have attempted to refine and redefine Jaspers's concept as "radical empathy" (Matthew Ratcliffe) and "second order empathy" (Giovanni Stanghellini) to address this limitation, but they do so by expanding rather than challenging an idea of empathy.[18]

Later in the century, in the United States, Carl Rogers pioneered a branch of therapy founded on the conviction that human well-being, growth, and healing could be forged in a therapeutic relationship of authenticity between two human persons. Rogers claimed that this relationship was characterized by "a sort of transparency on my [the therapist's] part, in which my real feelings are evident; by an acceptance of this other person as a separate person with value in his own right; and by a deep empathic understanding which enables me to see his private world through his eyes."[19] It is via the vulnerability of the therapist in the Rogerian encounter that the client is able to relate more truthfully and honestly, with "congruence," and to grow in confidence and self-regard. Rogers can be credited for the centrality accorded to the role played by empathy in many subsequent psychotherapeutic schools. In a reflection on the similarities between practices of feminist therapy and Rogers's person-centered model, for example, Laura S. Brown writes that "the centrality of empathy to psychodynamic practices," as insisted upon by Rogers, a pioneering gesture for his time, "has been established today."[20] She goes on to claim that this method is key for feminist therapy's "willingness to take a stance of respect and empathy for the experiences of someone who is socially and experientially 'other.'"[21]

Rogers insisted also that the therapist must hold the client in "unconditional positive regard," irrespective of his or her character, and "listen emphatically." These demands on the therapist for an unconditional degree of empathy, and for an attitude of unquestioning positivity toward the other, may place a burden on them which appears almost superhuman. Indeed criticisms of Rogers's precepts have included his tendency to see human nature in an immensely optimistic light—capable of infinite development and growth, if subject to an adequately positive relationship. The idea that no human being is sufficiently prey to dark and antisocial impulses as to be unreachable via therapy is a belief that, while perhaps heartwarming, is, in Kathleen O'Dwyer's words in her essay on Rogers as a "quiet revolutionary," "based on an unconventionally compassionate view of human nature."[22]

As empathy has become an object of contested definition for those in the psy sciences and for social commentators alike, subdefinitions have emerged as well as definitions of "good" and "bad" empathy. Kathryn Robson charts these developments,[23] pointing out that Coplan, for example, differentiates "pseudo-empathy" from "genuine empathy," where the former involves an ego-driven projection onto the other and the latter an attempt "to simulate the target individual's experiences."[24] Feminist scholar Clare Hemmings, meanwhile, has argued that "good empathy" is a recognition and witnessing of the other's condition, whilst "bad empathy" involves usurping the other's position and speaking for or in place of them.[25] And in recognition of this moral complexity, a branch of study known as "critical empathy" has emerged. Andrea Lobb distinguishes what she calls "doxic empathy" (from Pierre Bourdieu's *doxa*—that which is a cultural given and reifies social power dynamics) from "critical empathy,"[26] a form of reflexive empathy that pays attention to the power inherent in empathic dynamics, both peer-to-peer and in professional and clinical settings, "as a politicized adaptation of the psychoanalytic method of listening."[27] What underpins all of the assessments of empathy briefly summarized above is the shared belief that empathy—if done well, or properly, or thoroughly enough—remains an a priori good.

The Proponents of Empathy qua Panacea: de Waal and Baron-Cohen

More recently some vocal proponents of empathy have argued in crossover books that, beyond its usefulness in the clinical setting, empathy is the single good that redeems human social life. Two of the most prominent of these are Frans de Waal, a Dutch primatologist and ethologist based in the United States, and British psychologist Simon Baron-Cohen, whose positions I will discuss below.

De Waal published the emotively titled *The Age of Empathy: Nature's Lessons for a Kinder Society* in 2009. The work sets out to argue that "human empathy has the backing of a long evolutionary history."[28] De Waal counterposes "sympathy" and "fellow feeling" (both often subsumed in his work under the label "empathy") to the competitive principle of the market, arguing that the former run deep in our DNA and that we would be mistaken to assume as a truth an innate human tendency to prioritize the latter. He aims for a "complete overhaul of assumptions about human nature,"[29] replacing Plautus's proverb *homo homini lupus*, much cited by Thomas Hobbes, with evidence of a drive for collectivism that humans have allegedly inherited from primates. Yet the first three chapters of his book seem to argue more for the existence of a human tendency for *cooperation*, based on the behavior of our close animal cousins and ancestors, rather than for the "in-feeling" of empathy per se.

The specific character of empathy is finally attended to in chapter 4, titled—predictably—"Someone Else's Shoes." De Waal makes the bold claim that responses to others that are instinctively, rather than cognitively, rooted have a moral superiority. He writes: "Clearly, we often make snap judgments that come from 'the gut.' Our emotions decide, after which our reasoning power tries to catch up as a spin doctor."[30] The rhetoric is interesting. Emotions are "pure," while reason is allocated the function of "spin doctoring," not often seen as a noble endeavor. Primates do not have politics—their empathy is not expressed in the context of an ideology of virtue—so the atavistic nature of the empathic response makes it resonate as especially *authentic* here.

From an even more radically pro-empathy position, Simon Baron-Cohen sets out in his 2012 book to "understand human cruelty" by replacing the notion of "evil" with the concept of "empathy erosion."[31] While I have long been troubled by the overuse of the quasi-theological word "evil" to account for (banal, pace Hannah Arendt) human acts of violence and cruelty, and therefore would echo Baron-Cohen's wish to understand human ethics and those behaviors that violate widely shared human moral codes in a more secular manner, I cannot help but think that empathy is again charged with doing too much here. Also, the contention that "evil" is interchangeable with "zero degrees of empathy" is one that deserves some careful unpacking, lest it cast moral doubt on individuals with nontypical ways of functioning.

Baron-Cohen defines empathy as a "double-minded focus of attention," that is, one that involves "keeping in mind someone else's mind, at the very same time [as one's own]."[32] He delineates how being on the receiving end of someone's empathy *feels* (using the verb "to feel" a dizzying number of times) and adduces the value of empathy from this: "Empathy makes the other person feel valued, enabling them to feel their thoughts and feelings have been heard, acknowledged and respected."[33] While this might be so, the claims made for empathy become increasingly grandiose and unreasonable throughout his work: "Empathy avoids *any risk of misunderstandings or miscommunications*, by figuring out what the other person might have intended,"[34] he writes. With the best will in the world, apprehending another's feelings or intentions so perfectly could only be the result of a form of telepathy with supernatural overtones, rather than an ordinary sympathetic or identificatory human response. And, with similar hyperbole, he writes in the book's conclusion: "Empathy is like a universal solvent. Any problem immersed in empathy becomes soluble."[35]

Baron-Cohen goes on to identify categories of people who constitutionally lack empathy or have "zero empathy." The first category contains the people diagnosed as "personality disordered": the "borderline" type (Borderline Personality Disorder is now more frequently referred to as Emotionally Unstable Personality Disorder or EUPD); the "antisocial" type (or psychopath); and the "narcissist." Baron-Cohen suggests that the taxonomy of personality disorder (PD) is only partially useful, as it describes outward manifestations of "abnormality" but does not identify what he proposes the common underlying cause of these "disorders" to be: a dearth of empathy. It should be noted that, in very recent years, especially in British psychiatry, PD diagnoses tout court are subject to questioning as to their appropriateness and usefulness.[36] And for many years now, patient groups and psychiatrists have been pointing out the often unhelpfully stigmatizing nature of these labels, as well as the structural misogyny often present in diagnoses of Borderline/EUPD: it is a label mainly given to difficult or disagreeable, usually traumatized, women.[37] In attributing a single cause—empathy deficit—to all three very different "disorders" he names, Baron-Cohen risks conflating extremely varied phenomena and patient experiences. He is also, perhaps unwittingly, complicit in the social stigmatization of those diagnosed with PDs as he describes their shared "zero degree of empathy" as "clearly negative;"[38] while arguing that one other group that struggles with empathy may be viewed as "surprisingly positive":[39] those with the Autism Spectrum diagnoses, especially what used to be called Asperger Syndrome, who tend to be intelligent, sensitive, systematic thinkers who merely struggle with social and interpersonal cues. Baron-Cohen commits a serious logical and ethical error in his book: He draws no distinction between ascribing "negativity" (a word he states he is using, along with "empathy erosion," in place of "evil") to those diagnosed with Antisocial Personality Disorder, many of whom are violent criminals, most often men, *and* to those with the Borderline Personality Disorder (or EUPD) label, who are most usually young women in emotional distress, a disproportionate number of whom are survivors of childhood sexual abuse. If I shared Baron-Cohen's predilection for empathy, I might argue that this gesture marks a failure on his part to display that quality which he describes as "the *most valuable resource* in our world."[40] Conflating abuse survivors with likely perpetrators of violence, and designating both "evil," appears to demonstrate a marked lack of "feeling" for the latter. But I prefer to conclude instead that his judgment is poor in this respect, and that his adherence to his thesis that empathy is the sole prerequisite for absolute good leads to some—to say the least—ethically, as well as logically, dubious claims.

Against Empathy: Some Critiques

Having tarried with the works of some of those who seek to promote empathy as the superlative therapeutic tool, value empathy above all other moral mechanisms, and argue that it is an innate evolutionary property of (functional) humans as a species, we now turn to extant critiques of the concept and to alternative ethical and therapeutic modes of encountering the other.

In an article critical both of Karl Jaspers's original concept of empathy and subsequent redefinitions of it within the field, critical psychiatrists Lucienne Spencer and Matthew Broome argue against empathy on the grounds of both effectiveness and ethics. First they claim that "to overstate the level of insight the clinician can gain from any form of empathic understanding can lead to a misunderstanding and a misappropriation of a psychiatric condition."[41] Next they develop a critique of how a clinical focus on empathy can risk a particular kind of "epistemic injustice."[42] This term, coined by Miranda Fricker,[43] describes ways in which "someone is disingenuously downgraded and/or disadvantaged in respect of their status as an epistemic subject" or "knower."[44] Spencer and Broome coin the concepts of "epistemic co-opting" and "epistemic objectification," building on Fricker. They argue that "by overstating the clinician's ability to access the patient's lived experience . . . through the empathic approach, the clinician risks 'co-opting' the epistemic privilege of the marginalised subject."[45] Then they suggest that, despite being framed as relational, the empathic approach Jaspers advocated can result in the patient being mined as a (re)source for the clinician, rather than listened to as an authority on their own experience.

Moreover, as Spencer and Broom point out, while phenomenological psychopathology is committed to recognizing the power imbalance inherent to psychiatry (the very imbalance that Foucault drew to our attention in his *History of Madness*) and working toward mitigating it via the dialogic relation between clinician and patient, the insistence on empathy risks, in fact, being its ethical weak point. They go so far as to conclude that "empathic understanding is an aspect of the methodology that ought to be jettisoned in favour of approaches that champion the epistemic agency of the patient."[46] One example they give of such an approach is a form of "virtuous listening," again borrowing from Fricker, who conceptualizes this as a "proactive and socially aware kind of listening,"[47] which does not assume that the psychiatrist can directly access the patient's lived experiential world.

In his work on the moral case for empathy from the perspective of analytical philosophy, Jesse Prinz has argued that, while it is a good, empathy alone is not a suitable tool for ensuring morality.[48] He argues that, although it is pleasant to experience empathy for and from the other in the context of our friendships and family relationships, empathy is potentially damagingly limiting to the exercise of moral judgement. Arguing that empathy is insufficient, Prinz posits that we might prioritize instead "concern," a "cousin of empathy."[49] He describes it as "a fellow feeling that arises when we consider another's plight." Empathy for Prinz "is an emotion we share with another," whereas concern is "a negative sentiment caused by the recognition that someone is in need."[50] Concern is considered better than empathy by Prinz because it is not a form of "emotional mimicry."[51]

However, despite pointing to some of empathy's shortcomings if used as the sole and supreme moral arbiter, he does not suggest instead that morality should be grounded outside of purely affective terms as far as is possible. Indeed, Prinz seems very concerned that we should not judge *him* as unemotional: "At this point, you may be gritting your teeth and thinking that

I am a cold, heartless, and sanctimonious Millian monster who treats human beings as statistics. That is not my intention. I do not advocate a heartless morality. I have indicated that morality is emotionally grounded."[52] These words of mitigating coda add nothing of substance to his argument and read rather as an appeal to the spirit of the time, bespeaking an awareness of the importance of being seen to operate always in a mode that is affective.

Moving from the analytical philosophical field to the continental one, the thought of Talmudic scholar and philosopher Emmanuel Levinas offers a particularly striking critique of the idea of empathy as a good. Levinas's philosophy suggests an at once more subtle and more radical critique of empathy than that offered by analytical philosophy. Levinas's ethics is predicated on the notion of absolute respect for irreducible alterity. This formulation makes empathy ethically dubious, since it exemplifies the reduction of otherness to the same. In his *Totality and Infinity* of 1969, Levinas describes the Western philosophical quest for knowledge of the other as a kind of violence. For Levinas, the challenge of the encounter with the other is a challenge of absolute respect without making a claim for likeness to the self—perhaps the polar opposite of Carl Rogers's idea of an ethical encounter discussed above. By viewing empathy through a Levinasian lens, the compassion assumed to lie in empathy becomes instead violent reduction—what Levinas calls the "imperialism of the same."[53]

While at first glance the Levinasian objections to empathy may seem somewhat obscurantist in their theoretical formulation, in fact there are numerous studies in existence that have attempted to apply them in pragmatic real-world contexts, such as to the field of social worker training. In an article on how Levinasian alternatives to empathy might better shape training in this profession, Nai Ming Tsang points out that the caring and social work fields "always involve a tension between the dominant reliance on rationality, knowledge and skills and the urgent call for ethical commitment and the use of the practitioner's self."[54] She argues that Levinas's specific notion of *otherness* "challenges an overly optimistic view of empathy in social work"[55] while also demanding responsibility on the part of the social worker.

What is particularly important about Levinas's thought is that it offers an alternative solution to the question of ethically approaching the other that excludes and surpasses empathy. Pro-empathy writers tend to assume the human capacity for empathy as the definitional condition for ethical behavior toward the other, as when de Waal writes: "Asked why he never talked about the number of civilians killed in the Iraq War, U.S. defense secretary Donald Rumsfeld answered: 'Well, we don't do body counts on other people.' Empathy for 'other people' is the one commodity the world is lacking more than oil."[56] Levinas shows us that it is not necessarily empathy that lacks in this example. It is not necessary to stand in the shoes of those radically other to us in order to care about their humanity. For him it should, indeed, be their very irreducible difference from us that makes us concerned and responsible.

However it must be noted that Levinasian philosophy poses as a problem not only empathy, with its arrogantly reductive tendencies, but also the whole endeavor of seeking to *know* or *understand* the other. Tammy Amiel-Houser and Adia Mendelson-Maoz explain that "in Levinas's thinking, ethical relations with another person do not depend on knowledge or understanding, but instead involve a welcome of the unknown and the incomprehensible."[57] The rational desire to know is problematized alongside the supposition of in-feeling, as both are conceptualized as forms of reduction. Nai Ming Tsang's article about Levinasian approaches to social work training precisely draws attention to the perceived problem in that profession of assuming that the relationship between social work professional and service-user is one in which the former's role is primarily to understand what the other is feeling and why they are behaving in certain ways, therefore reducing them to an object of comprehension. But without any attempt to understand or to know, the social worker would be no more than a listener. Of course we should not ignore the value of listening (pace Spencer and Broome). However listening is only one component of a role that involves such pragmatic and cognitively complex considerations as assessing child-protection needs. While Levinas's rejection of the assumption of empathy's beneficence is refreshing, his suspicion of any kind of attempt to comprehend rationally the other's position poses grave limitations to the applicability of what is perhaps best seen as a beautiful thought experiment for real-world contexts.

Finally, then, I turn to a critic of empathy who believes that we need to look squarely to the operation of the rational order if we are to form a better system of ethics, including therapeutic ethics, the psychologist Paul Bloom. In his book *Against Empathy* of 2016, Bloom sets out precisely to argue why a world with less empathy and more rational compassion in it would be a better one. Like others discussed, he takes emotional empathy to mean the ability to "stand in someone else's shoes," or to feel their suffering as if it was one's own. Bloom provides several counterarguments against emotional empathy, claiming that it is, at best, morally neutral. He expounds the concept of "rational compassion" as an alternative to empathy, writing, "I want to make a case for the value of conscious, deliberative reasoning in everyday life, arguing that we should strive to use our heads rather than our hearts. We do this a lot already, but we should work on doing more."[58] This situating of human reason as a positive function places him almost directly counter to de

Waal's previously discussed assertion that gut feeling–issued empathy is an atavistic good, while interpretative reason is no more than a meddlesome spin doctor.

One of Bloom's most persuasive arguments contra empathy is the fact that many studies show that empathic responses often depend on the perceived similarity of the other person to the self, even for those with egalitarian political views. Bloom writes: "Intellectually, a white American might believe that a black person matters just as much as a white person, but he or she will typically find it a lot easier to empathize with the plight of the latter than the former."[59] People have also been shown to feel more moved by the plights of attractive, rather than unattractive, individuals, and by named or pictured individuals rather than groups. Empathy, by appealing to emotional triggers, also predicates responses on the basis of sentimental reactions that may fly in the face of considerations of fairness. Consider this example Bloom raises, quoted at length:

> C. Daniel Batson and his colleagues did an experiment in which they told subjects about a ten-year-old girl named Sheri Summers who had a fatal disease and was waiting in line for treatment that would relieve her pain. Subjects were told that they could move her to the front of the line. When simply asked what to do, they acknowledged that she had to wait because other more needy children were ahead of her. But if they were first asked to imagine what she felt, they tended to choose to move her up, putting her ahead of children who were presumably more deserving. Here empathy was more powerful than fairness, leading to a decision that most of us would see as immoral.[60]

Empathy, as the example of Sheri Summers suggests, often works precisely as a form of unconscious bias—that psychological mechanism which so many hours of corporate "Equality

Diversity and Inclusivity" training are spent teaching us to recognize and overcome. Bloom puts it thus: "Empathy distorts our moral judgments in pretty much the same way that prejudice does."[61] This characteristic of empathy reveals that not only does it sometimes fail to be an unalloyed good, but it also does not necessarily "do no harm" on a personal or social level.

Additionally, Bloom attends to the potential harm of empathy to the person doing the empathizing. He draws on a hypothetical empathic person sketched by Baron-Cohen, a therapist called Hannah who is hardwired "so that the experiences of others are always in her head—99 for everyone else and 1 for her."[62] Bloom points out firstly that it is not surprising that Baron-Cohen made his empath a woman, as women score more highly than men on a range of tests that measure "concern with others"—for explanatory reasons that would no doubt differ if one asked evolutionary psychologists and then asked radical feminists. Secondly he asks what the risks and costs of Hannah's empathic excesses would be to her. He makes clear that the problem is not that she cares, but that "her caring is driven by her receptivity to suffering."[63] We may think again here of Carl Rogers's ideal therapist whose own empathic vulnerability is his primary clinical tool. (I would bet my life savings that the hypothetical Hannah is a Rogerian.) Bloom offers evidence that those who feel others' suffering to excess are—perhaps unsurprisingly—susceptible to anxiety and eventually to burnout. He describes research experiments carried out by Tania Singer and her team in which participants were given training in techniques of either empathy or compassion.[64] The MRI scans of participants revealed different neural activity—activation of the insular and anterior cingulate cortex regions as a result of empathy training, and activation of the medial orbitofrontal cortex and ventral striatum after compassion training. The former brain regions are active when one is experiencing pain, the latter when decision-making.

Experientially, participants described finding empathy training (being asked to empathize with those who were suffering) "unpleasant," whereas compassion training (encouragement to feel kindly and lovingly toward the other) led both to "better feelings on the part of the meditator and kinder behavior."[65]

Bloom notes that, despite these findings, "empathy has been named an 'essential learning objective' by the Association of Medical Colleges."[66] He shares a letter he received, after publishing an article sketching his critique of empathy, from an emergency physician who attended the aftermath of the attack on the Twin Towers on 9/11. She writes to Bloom: "I not only opened myself up to trying to be there and feel the pain with the workers there, but I also tried to really take in my surroundings and feel the horror and loss around me. I felt it was somehow immoral not to. One day I was way too successful at being empathic in that way, and it was more than I could take."[67] Via this example and others, Bloom demonstrates, perhaps most convincingly of all the critical writers on this subject, the potential dangers of overvaluing empathy. These include both the lure of favoring those with whom one can most closely identify (or who appear most superficially attractive or sympathetic), and the risk of being overwhelmed with this feeling in a way that can lead to exhaustion, ill health, and a consequent paralysis of ethical action. Seen in this light, the affective overload of empathy can be better understood as a potential barrier to ethics, not its motor.

Feminism, Empathy, and Solidarity
(or I'll Mind My Own Shoes, but Keep an Eye on Yours)

One of my main concerns regarding empathy is the degree to which it is a heavily, if implicitly, gendered concept. My 2019 book *Selfish Women* concerned itself precisely with the ways in which half of the population has historically been conditioned to do the work of being selfless—and how this has rendered self-interested women, or those who are not predisposed toward empathy or care, largely culturally illegible and presumed unnatural. It is in a related vein that I argue here that the ongoing idealization of empathy poses a problem for redressing gendered and racialized stereotyping. In her work on "critical empathy," Lobb writes of the need to attend to how tropes of gender, as well as of class and race "mesh with cultural tropes of empathy. In effect, doing empathy is often deeply suffused with stereotyped expectations of doing gender, in the sense that the expectations, rewards, and costs of women's performance of empathy are demonstrably different from those of men."[68]

I am, frankly, concerned by the implications of idealizing empathy which—when reduced to its purest form, as in the example of Baron-Cohen's "Hannah"—is the *emptying out* of the self *for* the other—an echo of regressive traditional modes of female socialization. The gesture of elevating a virtue traditionally assumed to be feminine may be seen by some to be a feminist gesture in the "ethics of care" tradition,[69] and again, we may think of Mattel's claim that getting all kids to play with Barbies and Kens, a traditionally "feminine" play style, will make them all more empathic citizens. However, if a virtue ascribed to "the feminine" is no more valuable to the self or other—of either sex—than different virtues, perhaps those more traditionally presumed masculine, why would we attempt to elevate the (presumed) feminine, rather than redistribute the (presumed) masculine? Whom would this *serve*? This issue can be seen as a microcosm of the argument of the current book as a whole: It is not *necessarily* desirable or particularly liberating to revalorize those emotional attributes that have been presumed to belong properly to subordinate others; rather we may attain fairness and equality of opportunity for all by promoting and valuing the more pragmatically and demonstrably beneficial—again, for self and other—virtues and strategies.

That empathy arguably risks harm to the self as well as to the other is a point made powerfully by Bloom. As discussed above, he describes the mental pain and burnout experienced by highly empathic individuals. Empathy seen in this light is another form of, often gendered, emotional labor, and the refusal to privilege it may be unfairly interpreted as selfishness. Indeed Baron-Cohen uses "selfish" in the conventional, negatively connoted, way with regard to empathy: "Having zero degrees of empathy is ultimately a lonely kind of existence, a life at best misunderstood, at worst condemned as selfish."[70] In *Selfish Women*, I argued for the adoption of what I call ethical "self-fulness," which involves recognizing and retaining the self's boundaries and interests as an inviolable principle and value—but also as the precondition for meaningful solidarity.

A case study in action of this problem is discussed in Alexis De Coning's 2022 article that examines in the first person a feminist social science researcher's grappling with empathy as an ethical strategy when working with participants who are members of "unsavory populations."[71] In the particular case of her article, these are members of the so-called men's rights movement, some of whom she met and interviewed as a researcher at the International Conference on Men's Issues (ICMI) in 2019. De Coning emphasizes the commitment to empathy for one's participants that is the cornerstone of feminist standpoint theory and methodology. She grapples with the question of how to deploy strategies of critical empathy to avoid demonizing, dehumanizing, or projecting onto others whose values one does not share, while not violating one's own ethico-political convictions. By "critical empathy" she explains that she specifically means here trying to feel into the other's perspective while also being aware of the problematic feelings this brings up in herself. She discusses "sitting in that venue trying to 'feel with' the other attendees,"[72] while they scapegoated feminism as the source of men's supposed loss of purpose and power and increased sense of hopelessness. While the researcher does not abandon empathy as a tool altogether, she registers her own feelings of unease and frustration that surface and notes that "it is both the empathy and critique evoked by critical empathy that makes my investigation of the MRM possible, productive, and attendant to . . . nuances."[73] Yet, I wonder whether empathy, critical or not, is really the most appropriate tool for such an endeavor. Accepting that another person is human and worthy of respect on that basis, while disagreeing with them, should not have to be such an emotion-soaked undertaking. De Coning acknowledges the "gendered assumptions . . . where women are seen to embody the feminine virtue of empathy,"[74] but does not go so far as to call this virtue into question or to discard it as a dangerous ethic or flawed method for the feminist researcher. Indeed, the fact that the problems of empathy are obvious, but the potential rejection of it is so seemingly taboo, speaks to its dominion over our consciousness—and conscience.

Some Concluding Remarks

In the psychological thriller *Red Dragon* (Thomas Harris, 1981), the first novel in the popular Hannibal Lecter series, the protagonist and the antagonist are, respectively, an empath and a psychopath. Will Graham, the medically retired FBI agent who caught cannibal killer Lecter, is brought back into service to hunt down a serial killer who is committing home invasions and murdering families—the eponymous "Red Dragon." Graham is able to replay the actions of the killer in his mind because he can stand *as if in his shoes* and imagine his crimes. As one character says of Graham, "He can assume your point of view or mine—and maybe some other points of view that scare and sicken him.

It's an uncomfortable gift . . . Perception's a tool that's pointed on both ends."[75] Graham suffers deeply from what he is able, so easily, to feel in his imagination, as it is entirely repellent to his moral framework. Hannibal Lecter, on the other hand, can read (as the exemplary homonymic "*lector*") and understand Graham's inner torment, but feels no empathic suffering—he only experiences curiosity. It is, obviously, from an ethical point of view, better to be Will Graham than to be Hannibal Lecter, but in the narrative logic, Graham pays so high a mental and emotional price for his special skills that we cannot help but conclude it is much less painful (and more fun) to be Lecter. Paul Bloom writes as a disclaimer in the opening pages of *Against Empathy*, "This isn't one of those weird pro-psychopathy books,"[76] and I assure you that this is not a "weird pro-psychopathy" conclusion either. While I have chosen a rather whimsical (and obviously fictional) parable of an extreme empath and psychopath with which to begin tying up my various thoughts in this chapter, I also believe that it speaks to a critical truth that I want us to bear in mind: Too much ability *to feel into the other* risks doing us harm.

Why, then, is empathy so valued as an ethical mode in our current moment? Why should an ability to (imagine) insert(ing) myself into someone else's subjectivity be seen as a gesture of radical altruism, not one of projection or reduction? Why should "standing in someone else's shoes" be prioritized over standing *alongside* them or *solidarity*? I hold that it is precisely because it is such a profoundly affectively charged concept, in an epoch that elevates the ideal of feeling above all other values, that empathy comes freighted with excessive cultural approval. And yet, when "doing" empathy, in which one both obliterates the reality of the other in the service of an imaginary identification *and* distances oneself from the specific materiality of one's own interests in the present, one cannot properly do self-aware, other-respecting solidarity. In empathy, one violates both an ethic of self *and* an ethic of the other, pace Levinas. Where Prinz has suggested "concern" and Bloom "rational compassion," as better ethical models than emotional empathy, I return, again, to solidarity—what we might call *standing alongside someone different from myself, rather than standing in someone else's shoes*. This is, in fact, an ethico-political strategy that I consider to be an imperative in a world characterized dually by ever-tightening group identitarianism and growing intolerance of the other—as I shall go on to discuss in the next chapter.

3

Words as Weapons

The Tyranny of Vulnerability

When we claim to have been injured by language, what kind of claim do we make? We ascribe an agency to language, a power to injure, and position ourselves as the objects of its injurious trajectory. . . . Could language injure us if we were not, in some sense, linguistic beings, beings who require language in order to be?
—Judith Butler, *Excitable Speech*

I'm very proud that some people think I'm a danger for the intellectual health of students. When people start thinking of health in intellectual activities, I think there is something wrong. In their opinion I am a dangerous man, since I am a crypto-Marxist, an irrationalist, a nihilist.
—Michel Foucault, "Truth, Power, Self: An Interview"

This chapter looks at a particularly vexing element of what I am terming the *cultural affective turn* that is descended from and linked in multiple complex ways to its academic counterpart. The phenomenon in question is the distinctive rise of a particular deployment of the language of vulnerability and sensitivity in public discourse for moralistic, coercive, or silencing ends. The most often commented-upon example of this regards how forms of speech may or may or not be considered offensive, how "offense" can translate into "harm," and what may constitute reasonable means of avoiding the hurt feelings that issue from encountering speech. As examples, we are increasingly familiar with the concept of "safe spaces," and we have seen a rise in "no-platforming" strategies on university campuses in the United States, Canada, and the UK, in which individuals with what are deemed politically distasteful views are programmatically excluded from debate as their messages are transubstantiated from "distasteful" to "dangerous."

In *The Rise of Victimhood Culture* (2018), Bradley Campbell and Jason Manning argue that university students' "calls for trigger warnings and safe spaces . . . evince a strong tendency to emphasize victimization. . . . They are part and parcel of a language of victimhood that exaggerates harm and emphasizes vulnerability."[1] "Safe spaces," it is noted, can refer to at least two distinct ideas: firstly, officially designated areas, in which those belonging to marginalized groups can meet together, away from the larger population of an institution, and secondly, demands that the institution—for example, a university—as a whole must be made "safe," in the sense that students can exist there "without emotional discomfort."[2] No-platforming as a strategy dates back to the 1970s and its origins have been linked to the National Union of Students' attempts to block British National Front Party speakers from addressing university audiences.[3] The increase in frequency of such tactics over the past ten or twenty years—and the expansion of which views are considered "fascist-adjacent"—may be perceived either as an instance of improved accountability or as a threat to freedom of expression, depending on one's political and philosophical viewpoint. But either way, what it demonstrates is one particular instance of the creep of a manipulative deployment of affect into public and institutional life.

I would argue that it is especially useful to think about this development in the light of the discussion in chapter 1 of Sedgwick's influential "turn," since the refusal to debate "offensive" or "hurtful" counter-positions, and the move instead to retreat from rational discourse and into the realms of safe spaces to protect vulnerable feelings, can be seen precisely as a manifestation of the move from aggressive "critique" to defensive "repair." Whatever else it presages, and whatever its merits and demerits, this cultural phenomenon marks a striking sea change from the Enlightenment episteme to the episteme of affect. However it is not entirely accurate to locate the origin of belief in linguistic harm *solely* in the context of the affective turn. It would be more accurate to say that over the past thirty or so years, since the turn to affect, we have witnessed an *intensification* of this belief and an *emotional overlay* onto an idea already present in intellectual life since at least the 1970s.

That words are accorded enormous power is the legacy, in fact, of the "linguistic turn" that structuralism and post-structuralism heralded, in which the notion that language was omnipresent and constitutive—"il n'ya pas de hors-texte,"[4] ("there is nothing outside the text") in Derrida's much-quoted (and oft-misconstrued) words—gives rise to the philosophical conditions in which verbal insults may be understood as the equivalence of a fist to the jaw. Sociologist Pierre Bourdieu offered the understanding that the ills of inequality in Western democracies are produced and maintained less by physical force than by symbolic domination. He understands language as "an instrument of power and action" as much as a tool of communication.[5] In line with the intensification of sensitivity noted above, in recent years what would once have been understood technically as "symbolic violence" is now often termed, especially on social media, "literal violence." This marks both the colloquial slippage in meaning of the word "literal" to signify its exact opposite: "figurative" or "symbolic" (e.g. "I'm so tired, I'm literally dead"), and the notion that what touches our values—or, more often these days, our identity—threatens our very existence.

In *Excitable Speech* (1997), Judith Butler offers an argument for the exact equivalence of linguistic harm and literal harm. The first quotation in the epigraph of this chapter, taken from the opening page of that work, sets out the stakes of the claim, arguing that we could not be hurt by language were we not "in some sense, linguistic beings, beings who require language in order to be."[6] Yet it is significant that the recent tendency to avoid difficult and potentially hurtful debate altogether as a strategy of harm reduction is not what was proposed during the very height of the poststructuralist moment, when it was first assumed that "linguistic beings" were precisely what we were (in fact, sometimes, *all* that we were), but has become the default setting following the affective turn. Foucault's dual arguments that power is discursive and that we cannot escape from the forcefield of power, for example, did not lead him to argue for less discourse in political contexts but rather for strategic and heuristic counter-discourse—that is, for more speech. His spirited statement regarding welcoming the "danger" attributed to his own speech and (projected) politics in the second citation of my epigraph shows the significant shift that has occurred. *Something* has happened on the intellectual left that has made us increasingly wary of disobedient opinions and of free speech as a value—until recently a staunchly leftist value.[7]

Yet, it is crucial to note that features of these tactics, perhaps homegrown by the left, are mirrored and pursued by some on the right. In *The Cultural Politics of Emotion*, Sara Ahmed, also pointing out the profound affective turn we have undergone, has written pertinently that in our current moment, "the hierarchy between emotion and thought/ reason gets displaced . . . into a hierarchy between emotions," whereby some emotions are elevated as "high" while others are coded "low."[8] I would add that it will depend on the political affiliation of those doing the coding as to which are valorized or deprecated and in which contexts. She also points out the deployment of a "soft"/"hard" taxonomy, echoing Tomkins-via-Sedgwick on emotions. Taking as an example the far right in Britain, Ahmed writes, "Emotions, for the British National Front, may pose a danger to the national body of appearing soft," for example, soft on immigration, soft on law and order.[9] But, as she also pertinently points out, "The narrative itself is an emotional one... *Hardness is not the absence of emotion but a different emotional orientation towards others.*"[10] While juxtaposing their "hardness" to a flaccid "softness," the right nevertheless makes emotional appeals of vulnerability when talking of taking measures to—for example—secure borders to ensure safety and protection.

This example will likely be as familiar to those in the United States and Canada as to those in the UK, but such phenomena are not only seen in the Anglosphere. Over the past ten years, resurgent hard-right-wing nationalisms in Central and Eastern Europe have been making increasing appeals to fear and hatred of the other, weaponizing feelings of xenophobia, misogyny, homophobia, and transphobia via deceptively defensive rhetoric. In Hungary in particular, Viktor Orbán's populist government imposed a ban on the teaching of gender studies in public universities under the claim that it poses a threat to "our children"[11] and to traditional family values; as a result, George Soros's Central European University, where I was recently honored to be a visiting speaker, has been forced to relocate to Vienna, Austria. This is a clear instance of the authoritarian closing-down of free speech by the populist far right on the grounds of emotional appeal. We have seen (bravely thwarted) governmental attempts to implement similar measures in Romania and increased persecution and erosion of legal protection for LGBTQ+ people in Poland until very recently. Northern Europe has not escaped. In The Netherlands—that longtime bastion of liberalism—far-right leader Gert Wilders recently won an election and Marine Le Pen, the leader of the *Front national*, came unprecedentedly close to doing likewise in France, while elections in Germany revealed gains for Alternative für Deutschland.

Daniel Albertazzi and Duncan McDonald have described right-wing populist rhetoric in the twenty-first century as that which "pits a virtuous and homogeneous people against a set of elites and dangerous 'others' who are together depicted as depriving (or attempting to deprive) the sovereign people of their rights, values, prosperity, identity and voice."[12] In these national(ist) examples the dangerous "other" is embodied in the figure of the migrant, the feminist, the LGBTQ+ person, or the left-wing intellectual, who apparently poses threats to the "traditional values" or "family values" of the "native" population. It is especially noteworthy for us that it casts the latter as vulnerabilized, often by relying on the figure of the child and the notion of indigenous (white) populations under the threat of eradication. "Vulnerability," in fact, has been reified and weaponized *across* the political spectrum to become a transcendental signifier of virtue, while offensive speech has been concretized as the vice of "literal violence."

Who May Critique Vulnerability?

It bears noting that many published critiques of the phenomenon of increased sensitivity and a culture of rhetorical victimhood that I have sketched above already exist, but that they tend to focus solely on the problem of left-wing instances of this phenomenon—on condemnations of what is dismissively termed "snowflakery," "grievance," or "wokeness"—and to ignore the manipulative deployment of emotive language by the right. Such critiques issue generally, though not always, from conservative or classical liberal perspectives and, in the interest of balance, I will discuss below three key works of this kind written from different political standpoints.[13]

One of the best-known studies of this topic that issues from a staunchly conservative perspective is *The Coddling of the American Mind* (2018) by Greg Lukianoff and Jonathan Haidt. This work sets out to explore three perceived untruths that the authors claim dominate our epoch: "fragility" (what doesn't kill you makes you weaker), "emotional reasoning" (always trust your feelings), and "us versus them" (life is a battle between good people and evil people). The authors contend that a generation of young people is being brought up to believe these three affective untruths, resulting in mental health crises, uniformity of thinking, and a peer-policing culture among the current generation of students. They point out that, while students have always protested speakers and ideas that they find dangerous or repellent, the past twenty years have seen a shift from protest on the grounds of moral or political opposition to claims "that certain kinds of speech . . . interfered with their *ability to function*,"[14] and that the "community would be *harmed* by the speaker's visit."[15]

Lukianoff and Haidt ask whether "safety versus danger [is] a helpful framework" for considering ideas in universities—and in broader culture—and conclude that it is not.[16] Their book proposes, as an antidote to the domination of emotional functioning, the harnessing of techniques of cognitive behavioral therapy designed to avoid catastrophizing and to build "resilience" (a word that has become, in left-wing scholarship, a byword for neoliberal agendas).[17] I confess I find this a bizarrely narrow and arbitrary sinecure for such a multicausal and complex phenomenon. Further, what this critique, like many of its kind, also does is ascribe the prioritization of vulnerability solely to young people on the left, such that it becomes a partisan and generational attack, without noting that parallel strategies with equal force and opposite content have been and are being deployed from and by the right—often with "strong man" figureheads such as Orbán paradoxically voicing the rhetoric of the vulnerable.

Perhaps the work of this broad kind that comes closest to my critique and that offers the most nuance, while not entirely sharing my methodological or theoretical commitments, is that offered by self-defined classical liberal writers Helen Pluckrose and James Lindsay in *Cynical Theories* (2020). Herein the authors note, as do I, that liberal democracy is under threat from "two overwhelming pressures, one revolutionary and the other reactionary."[18] These are: far-right populist movements, who are "increasingly turning toward leadership in dictators" and "far-left progressive social crusaders" who "reject liberalism as a form of oppression . . . with increasingly authoritarian means."[19] Pluckrose and Lindsay go on to state that "While the problem to the right is severe . . . we have become experts in the nature of the problem on the left."[20] Their self-declared "expert" analysis of how this state of affairs has come about lays the blame at the door of postmodernism and its creep from the academy to public and bureaucratic realms.

A logical leap is made between postmodernism's questioning of the grand narratives of modernity and the pursuit of what Pluckrose and Lindsay term (uppercase) "Social Justice" projects that reify certain groups and identities as unimpeachable victims, though the exact pathway from one to the other, and the many points of philosophical inconsistency between them, are not accounted for. The authors argue that the best cure for the ills of the current iteration of the left is a return to core liberal values including freedom of speech and a new universalism that is less focused on identity groupings. In fact,

I do not disagree particularly with this proposition as one valid redress; I have undertaken critique of the divisiveness of "identity politics" and reified "hierarchy of oppression"–style left-wing projects elsewhere,[21] and I am more sympathetic to liberal philosophical tenets than many of my theoretical humanities peers. But I dissent from the authors' claim that liberal ideals and postmodernism-inflected theories are "almost directly at odds with one another."[22] Indeed I am convinced that *without a nuanced analysis of power relations*, such as that offered by Foucault, any call for a return to pure liberalism may be a toothless one that will replicate the very issues within liberalism's origins that led to disenchantment with it. Without feminist and race-aware analysis, liberalism risks continuing to privilege white men as *the* a priori rational subjects. My argument here, and throughout this book, is that the tools of Modern Critical Theory in their critical—or hermeneutically suspicious—mode can *help* to overcome the excesses of the episteme of affect and its mapping onto identity categories with which we are presently afflicted, rather than serve as merely the inaccurately scapegoated origin of this ill.

Indeed the main argumentational weakness of *Cynical Theories*, for me, is that it fails to take onboard the decisive impact of the affective turn in theory and culture on the phenomena it discusses, a turn of which Pluckrose and Lindsay indeed seem entirely unaware, as the word "affective" does not feature anywhere in their book. The phenomena they describe would have been unlikely to take the *particular flavor* of coercive, emotive, manipulative, guilt-inducing moralism they have acquired—and that the authors decry—had the background environment been one soaking in reasoned critique rather than in affect. Indeed, in using the term "cynical" in place of "critical" in their book's title, they highlight a misguided attack on suspicious critique, which makes nonsense of their own skepticism of what they call "gnostic 'epistemologies' that rely upon feeling, intuition, and subjective experience,"[23]—which are quite obviously affect-turn-driven knowledge modes, the condemnation of which makes no sense without an acknowledgement of that phenomenon.

The final book with a not dissimilar argument that I will discuss in this section is *Left is Not Woke*, published in 2023 by Susan Neiman who defines herself as a left-wing thinker. Neiman states the difficulty of critiquing, or even of using, the word "woke" as a left-wing writer, recalling, "Many colleagues urged me not to criticize the woke at all, for fear that any critique would be instrumentalized by the right."[24] She argues that "woke" describes a deformation of left-wing projects that once shared ideals of universalism rather than tribalism, justice rather than power analysis, and progress rather than defeatist pessimism. These have been sacrificed in current times, she argues, in favor of identity-driven projects "built on a clash between feeling and thought"[25] in which "concern for marginalized persons [ends] by reducing each to the prism of her marginalization"[26] and in which "the parts of identities that are most marginalized [are] multiplied into a forest of trauma."[27] As well as restating the victimhood claims discussed by Lukianoff and Haidt and by Pluckrose and Lindsay, Neiman argues that victimhood is effectively *celebrated* in woke politics, commenting that the "burgeoning academic discipline called 'Memory Studies' is almost entirely dedicated to bad memories. While we once neglected to honor history's victims, we are now in danger of forgetting her heroes."[28]

A review of Neiman's work by Samuel Huneke for the *Los Angeles Review of Books* takes issue with her claims to be making a "leftist" rather than liberal argument,[29] but Neiman ripostes adamantly in a letter in response to that review that she has settled this issue in the introduction of her book, by adding to a list of principles shared by socialists and liberals ("freedoms to speak, worship, travel and vote") a uniquely leftist one: "Social rights, which undergird the real exercise of political rights" and which liberals would dismiss as "benefits, entitlements or safety nets."[30] One feature that Neiman's book certainly shares with that of liberals Pluckrose and Lindsay, however, is a tendency to blame the described state of affairs on "theory," leading with Foucault. But Neiman goes even further—in fact so far as to propose that Foucault's suspicious pessimism of the idea that progress can be devoid of power relations should be understood as a "nihilism" which leads us to a position that is "not far enough from" fascistic thinking, via a comparison with Nazi political theorist Carl Schmitt.[31] Foucault-as-ubiquitous-cultural-bogeyman is a tiresome, much-used trope that I have unpacked elsewhere, but most usually he is accused of moral relativism or sexual immorality by the right and of being too fascinated with the early iterations of neoliberalism by the left, rather than of Nazi-adjacency.[32] Neiman is—even more so than I am—a programmatic defender of the potential and value of Enlightenment thinking; indeed she has made this the entire focus of her illustrious career. But she opposes to the Enlightenment mode the strange triumvirate of Foucault, Schmitt, and the whole field of evolutionary psychology, rather than the affective turn which is, I am proposing, its most obvious recent foil. Neiman simplifies and fundamentally misconstrues Foucault's attitude toward Enlightenment. I agree with the book's reviewer Huneke when he writes: "At its best, Enlightenment thought teaches us to be skeptical of received wisdom, to question sources of power and structures of domination. This is precisely what the Foucauldian inheritance teaches too."[33]

I clearly do not wish to conflate or collapse the distinct agendas of the various above-discussed works, as I have shown that each issues from a different political viewpoint. However two of these books (Pluckrose and Lindsay's, and Neiman's) unite under a scapegoating of the names of critical theory as influencers of the current zeitgeist, particularly Foucault, often without a sound understanding of the philosophies in question and without any awareness of the move from critique to affect in that broader field. And what all three works focus on, in common with my current project, is the shared idea of a reification of victimhood status as a contemporary political resort. This makes me think also of Wendy Brown's Nietzschean work on "the wound" in *States of Injury* (1995), in which she argues, more sympathetically than the authors discussed above, that subaltern subjects may end up fetishizing the idea of injury to such a degree that the wound becomes the locus for their identity itself.[34] I propose to call this broad phenomenon "the Tyranny of Vulnerability," a seeming oxymoron which precisely suggests that vulnerability is both held as a high value, as Neiman argues, and/but is also weaponized in order to manipulate others into guilty silence or fearful compliance. It *has* to be possible to question and critique this strategy, weaponized by both left and right (although considered *only* in its leftist manifestations in the books discussed above), without suggesting agreement with cultural conservatives, antifeminists, neotraditionalists, or those engaged in knee-jerk intergenerational attacks—which themselves are often deeply emotive and manipulative in kind.

Jordan the Lobster King, Meet Judith the Giant of Gender

In this section I will consider in some detail two case studies issuing from diametrically opposed political and philosophical positions: examples of the writing and broadcasting of the Canadian evolutionary psychologist Jordan Peterson and Judith Butler's recent book entitled *Who's Afraid of Gender?* (2024). My aim is to show that these unlikely bedfellows employ some similar techniques including appeals to deliberately emotive language in place of evidenced argument, a deployment of the Tyranny of Vulnerability discourse, and avoidance of nuance to strengthen their rhetorical positions. Also, while Peterson and Butler may be politically and philosophically at opposing ends of a spectrum, their status as "intellectual celebrities" is a shared characteristic that gives their public-facing statements a certain power.

Jordan Peterson came to prominent public attention in 2016 for objecting to "compelled speech" in Canada's C-16 Bill on the grounds that he understood it to violate principles of free speech and to criminalize those in public life refusing to use the personal pronouns any individual requests.[35] He is an example of someone who nominally critiques manifestations of leftist identity politics and academic production on the grounds that they are rooted in emotion (calling himself a classical liberal but displaying undeniably social-conservative tendencies) yet who simultaneously writes and performs in the most overtly affective ways imaginable, as noted by Ben Burgis, one author of a cowritten book offering leftist critiques of Peterson. This makes Peterson a particularly stark example of the phenomenon under consideration. I will quote Burgis on this matter at length:

> If you've watched any significant portion of Peterson's YouTube videos, you shouldn't have any trouble imagining what he'd be like as either a New Age shaman or an evangelical protestant preacher. He's an electrifying speaker even—maybe *especially*—when he's saying absurd things. That's why he can tell a classroom full of adults in one video that "although it's hard to explain," he thinks that the twinned snake imagery in ancient artwork represents the DNA Double Helix discovered in the twentieth century. There's no nervous laughter because everyone in the room is swept up in his lecture. . . . When he gets teary talking about (extremely poorly-defined)

Words as Weapons

threats to "the individual" in another, no one looks away in embarrassment. The reason is that, at least for people who start out with neutral or positive feelings about Peterson, the emotional intensity helps sell his message.[36]

Slavoj Žižek, the maverick Slovenian Marxist-Lacanian—himself a critic of identity politics and "political correctness"—who debated Peterson in a battle of the phalluses in 2019, has also noted that Peterson "combines common sense and (the appearance of) cold scientific argument with a bitter rage."[37] As such Peterson is a perfect cipher of how the overuse of emotion-as-propaganda is not reducible to the left of politics: Peterson, if anything, is the Tyrant of Vulnerability in Chief. He is a particularly vocal opponent of Modern Critical Theory's influence on public discourse, referring often not only to the "cultural Marxism" often used as an empty catchphrase by members of the so-called alt-right but also to his own coining, "postmodern neo-Marxism," which, as we will explore, is something of an empty signifier.

Judith Butler, owing to the publication of their book *Gender Trouble* in 1990, is credited along with Eve Sedgwick with the "founding" of queer theory. (Sedgwick's *Epistemology of the Closet* appeared in the same year.) Butler is additionally often singled out as a key proponent of the jargonistic, obscurantist, and impenetrable quality of writing in the postmodern critical theoretical mode that Peterson attacks (in common with Pluckrose and Lindsay as well as Neiman). Indeed liberal analytical philosopher Martha Nussbaum famously dubbed Butler "the Professor of Parody" in a 1999 article of that name that critiques Butler's style as a symptom of the "tendency to regard the philosopher as a star who fascinates, and frequently by obscurity, rather than as an arguer among equals."[38] Nussbaum reminds us that Butler won the first prize in the inaugural annual Bad

Writing Contest sponsored by the journal *Philosophy and Literature* in 1998 and, indeed, the winning extract quoted therein reads as incomprehensible waffling. However in *Who's Afraid of Gender?*[39] Butler writes in a much less dense and technical style than in their earlier works, with the aim, presumably, of appealing precisely to nonacademics who may have become aware of a heated debate in feminism and cultural discourse more broadly regarding the ontological status of sex and gender that Butler wishes to illuminate from a particular perspective.

Peterson similarly wrote a book aimed at a popular market, *12 Rules for Life: An Antidote to Chaos* (2018), which became a multi-million-dollar bestseller, after his public opposition to C-16 Bill rocketed him to fame. He had earlier published only a single academic tome, *Maps of Meaning: The Architecture of Belief*, in 1999. The media circus surrounding *12 Rules* was followed by a benzodiazepine-withdrawal crisis, public breakdown, and slow recovery during which Peterson wrote its sequel, *Beyond Order: 12 More Rules*, which appeared in 2021. Most recently Peterson has disseminated (via his YouTube channel which, at the time of writing, has 8.2 million followers, as well as via a series of expensive, sold-out, international lecture tours) his thoughts on the lessons of Christianity as publicity for his fourth book, *We Who Wrestle with God* (2024).

The original *12 Rules for Life* appeals precisely to the feelings of inadequacy, resentment, and lack assumed to be experienced by the demographic shown to be most attracted to his work—young, white, North American men. Peterson argues in this book nominally in favor of a robust, no-nonsense, bootstrapping individualism: "Stand up straight with your shoulders back" is Rule 1, and "Set your house in perfect order before you criticize the world" (often summarized as "Tidy your bedroom") is Rule 2. He is strident in his claim that one must not scapegoat structural social inequality for personal failures—critiques of capitalism and patriarchy are dismissed as fallacious, and dominance hierarchy is held up as a natural, evolutionary condition that should not only be accepted but embraced, so long as it relies on competence, since it is "a near-eternal aspect of the environment, and much of what is blamed on these more ephemeral manifestations is a consequence of its unchanging existence."[40] However, rather than relying on the advocacy of reason that he claims to espouse herein, his book manipulatively characterizes the distinction between the responsible, continent, proud masculinity to which these young men should aspire—which he seems to be believe is their birthright by the law of Nature—and the "chaotic feminine," which is used to inspire revulsion in them.

At first we may, charitably, be willing to suppose that Peterson is talking about historical and symbolic ideas rather than actual men and women. He writes as an example of chaos that it is "what emerges . . . when you suddenly find yourself without employment, or are betrayed by a lover. As the antithesis of symbolically masculine order, it's presented imaginatively as feminine."[41] Yet a closer look at his rhetoric reveals a more literal intention. In discussing traditional gender roles and heterosexual complementarity, he claims: "It may be that only the woman who wants (or has) a child needs a man to rescue her—or at least to support and aid her. In any case, it is certain that a woman needs consciousness to be rescued, and . . . *consciousness is symbolically masculine and has been since the beginning of time* (in the guise both of order and of the Logos, the mediating principle)."[42] One of my arguments in this book is precisely that the virtues that have been traditionally coded masculine, such as reason, may indeed be more liberatory and beneficial for all individuals than the ones coded feminine, such as empathy. However, it is precisely my contention that all virtues are potentially proper to all subjects and that they were coercively, falsely, and manipulatively ascribed to dominant and oppressed subject positions respectively. Peterson appears instead to believe that the historical ascription *is* natural, evoking here *actual women* who may or may not want children and male protectors, *as well as* an idea of "symbolically" masculine or feminine traits that map onto them. While nominally appealing to science and reason, he repeatedly falls back on references to myth, spiritual psychology, and Jungian archetypes to argue for a transcendental and unchanging gendered essence.

Where Peterson does draw on science, it is to take some of the most fanciful examples from evolutionary psychology and biology. The most baroque of these, and one that has been much parodied, is his claim that the lobster, with which we share common if ancient genetic ancestry, offers an instructive analogy to the human since both lobster and human societies are founded on hierarchy. Moreover, a lobster who loses a fight will be much more likely to lose his next fight too, as a diminished dose of feel-good chemicals are released in his nerve endings as a result of defeat (lobsters, unlike humans, do not have brains), reducing confidence. Commentators have been quick to point out the far-fetched nature of the analogy. In a review of *12 Rules* for the *Times Literary Supplement*, Kate Manne muses humorously on the sheer oddness of asking us—or at least Peterson's male readers—to identify with the lobster "based on a supposedly shared obsession with territory and status (and also something about serotonin that seemed question-begging)."[43] Pointing out the problem of eliding the distinction between the concept of hierarchy and that of social power, Žižek has written, "There is no such authority in nature: lobsters have hierarchy but the top lobster among them has no *authority*; he rules by force, but he does not *exert power* in the human sense."[44]

Moreover, Peterson's robust assertions regarding the importance of looking to the agency of the self and not blaming systems are rather damningly contradicted and undercut when we turn to his critique of feminism—which is a masterclass in both blaming a system and mischaracterizing it. Feminism, for Peterson, appears to describe little more than a series of targeted attacks on men's freedoms (or historically accustomed dominance), as seen in Rule 11, which, while nominally about the importance of "not bothering children when they are skateboarding," contains a screed on how men are emasculated via feminized school systems, university settings, and workplaces. It is this feminization, according to Peterson, that has caused men to become increasingly fascinated by "harsh, fascist political ideology,"[45] in a masterly lesson in both victim blaming and scapegoating. As Marion Trejo has pointed out in her work on Peterson and feminism, "He makes sure to emphasize how men have it worse: from the decrease of men in tertiary education to the number of men in the army dying violent deaths"[46] and "There is an underpinning male victim logic: men suffer because feminists altered the natural order of things. Feminism is dangerous to all, but is most dangerous to men."[47] Speaking about "Gender, Patriarchy and the Slide towards Tyranny" on a podcast with Anne McElvoy for Intelligence Squared in 2018, the year of publication of *12 Rules*, Peterson stated that feminism is a "somewhat reprehensible ideology" and a "story fundamentally predicated on resentment."[48] Yet despite his own evident, blistering resentment of a feminism that he perceives to be harming boys and men, he does not acknowledge his *emotional* investment in this viewpoint and attempts to pass it off as a reaction based on reason. Boys and men emerge as the vulnerable victims of the devouring "feminine"—the titular "chaos" to which the *12 Rules* are an "antidote"—in this rather Gothic fantasy narrative.

A parallel target to feminism for Peterson's ire is poststructuralist or postmodernist thought, which he, like Pluckrose and

Lindsay and like Neiman, holds responsible for the recent fashion for identity politics—in which he includes feminism—and which he dubs "postmodern neo-Marxism." In the debate with Žižek, when pressed on what this term actually means and who its proponents might be, Peterson claimed: "I see the connection between the postmodernist types and the Marxists as a sleight-of-hand that replaced the notion of oppression of the proletariat by the bourgeois by the oppression by one identity group by another."[49] Žižek's response at this point was to agree with Peterson's analysis, but it is noteworthy that Peterson declined to name any "postmodern neo-Marxists." As Conrad Hamilton has pointed out in response to Peterson's claims, "Identity politics, of course, is not *the same thing* as poststructuralism—even if the former's denial of the possibility of experience outside a hermeneutic frame is partly derived from the latter."[50] Moreover the figures of French philosophy whom Peterson must have in mind, even as he does not name them, when making broad brush stroke claims about poststructuralism's influence on intellectual and political life—such as Foucault and Derrida—were not, in fact, "Marxists." I think again of the quotation in my epigraph, in which Foucault mockingly reels off the labels often used for him that make him "dangerous": "a crypto-Marxist, an irrationalist, a nihilist." And Hamilton accurately contends that, in fact, Peterson fundamentally misunderstands such thinkers, since Derrida, as I discussed in my introduction, "remained a defender of the rationalizing legacy of the Enlightenment—even if the defense of this legacy paradoxically required undermining many of its presuppositions."[51] This is, of course, an altogether more nuanced—and reasoned—position than Peterson's, which appears to hold that the side of rationality is any side he places himself on.

Turning now to Butler's 2024 book, the climate and circumstances that they describe as leading them to write it bear noting.

On a 2017 conference trip to São Paulo, Brazil, Butler found themself confronted by a group of far-right activists carrying an effigy with Butler's face on it.[52] This they proceeded to burn while chanting slogans that translated to "Less Butler, more family" and "Burn the witch."[53] At the airport in that same city, Butler and their partner were subjected to attempted physical assault. According to a petition signed by 370,000 Brazilian people, Butler's ideas were believed to pose a threat to "the natural order of gender, sexuality and the family."[54] In light of this, it is understandable that Butler felt that *Who's Afraid of Gender?* demanded to be written.

I was obviously immediately struck by the fact that Butler chose an emotional signifier—"fear"—and placed it into the rhetorical framing of "Who's afraid . . . ?" for their title. Firstly this formulation echoes the children's folkloric refrain "Who's afraid of the Big Bad Wolf?," suggesting a bogeyman function that the ideas of "gender," "gender ideology," by extension trans people, and finally Butler qua both individual and author name, are understood to occupy—as evidenced luridly in the São Paulo encounter. Indeed in the book "gender" is accorded the status of a "phantasm," a word Butler uses more than a hundred times throughout, as one reviewer notes,[55] to point to an imaginary signifying container of potent fearful affect. Secondly the interrogative "Who?" of the title suggests that the book's contents will offer an analysis of the positionality of those charged with doing the fearing. Yet, in the introduction, Butler describes an international, neofascist, "anti-gender ideology movement" that "treats gender as a monolith, frightening in its power and reach."[56] With chapters on the Vatican, Trumpian United States, and so-called TERF (trans-exclusionary radical feminist) groups in the UK, *Who's Afraid of Gender?* risks likewise treating the number of disparate players it critiques as a "monolith," despite occasionally noting that "the movement" does not take "a single form."⁵⁷ Framing the issue as one of *all* critics simply "being afraid of" gender means that both far-right traditionalists or populists and those feminists with different views about the ontological status and rights claims of "gender identity" and "biological sex" are assumed to be acting out of the same motives and as a result of the same kind of ignorant fear.

In a recent article criminologist Sarah Lamble, themself a pro-trans scholar in the UK, has carefully shown how Butler's zeal to make their argument has led to a fundamental error of fact: Many—though not all—"gender critical feminist" groups in the UK are on the left of politics, rendering the notion that this is a monolithic far-right-wing phenomenon wholly problematic.⁵⁸ Lamble cautions "against a simple conflation of gender critical feminism with right-wing politics and neo-fascism."⁵⁹ While some individuals and groups in the UK espousing "gender critical" views may indeed lean right, unlike in the United States, these are the minority. Butler claims that, while interested in the "materiality" of sex, gender critical feminists are not "generally materialist in a Marxist sense."⁶⁰ However, again, this is not necessarily true in the context of the UK. It bears noting that the British Communist Party currently takes a gender critical, sex-class-based stance. A statement on their website reads: "The Communist Party is the only political party with a coherent political analysis of sex and gender. Gender as an ideological construct should not be confused or conflated with the material reality of biological sex. Gender is the vehicle through which misogyny is enacted and normalised. Gender identity ideology is well-suited to the needs of the capitalist class, focusing as it does on individual as opposed to collective rights, enabling and supporting the super-exploitation of women."⁶¹ While Butler is of course at liberty to disagree with this characterization of gender, they cannot accurately claim it is a far-right one. Butler's lack of awareness of the national context reveals, at best, an ignorance of the UK's politics and an (unconscious?) assumption—hardly an error committed by Butler alone among American authors and academics—that all political scenes imitate the shape of the one in the United States. At worst, though, it suggests an attempt simply to dismiss those leftist feminists with whom Butler disagrees on this particularly charged question of identity as "fascists." In a recent book on the tension between "critique" and "tradition" in contemporary sex and gender rights movements in the UK, Darren Langridge has argued that "if we are to move beyond mere shouting, we need to stop calling people fascists, and TERF has become a term used in that manner."[62]

In a generally positive review of Butler's book for the *Chicago Review of Books*, Keith Contorno points out that Butler's reliance on the notion of "gender" as a "phantasm" means that "the phantasm itself becomes a catch-all, which works less as a tool to parse rhetoric than to create it—serving as a one-word dismissal of experiences and fears as fantasy." And by logical extension, this can be seen to disregard other "lived truths in the same manner that Butler says occurs when transgender experience is disregarded."[63] In dismissing *any* feminist concerns about changes to the official status of sex and gender—including demands for mere discussion—as symptoms of fearful neurosis, it is at least implicitly suggested (by the pervasive and persistent ghost of binary thinking's logic, as previously discussed) that Butler assumes the position they are taking against these enemies is one wholly on the side of reason. On this point, I find myself somewhat in sympathy with Pluckrose and Lindsay when they ask, in an epistemological moment that relies only on subjective claims of authority through appeal to emotional vulnerability, "What should we do when people's subjective experiences conflict?"[64] They note: "You have 'your truth,' and I have 'my truth,' and, when those diverge, there is no means of resolution. All we can do is each turn to our sect, the people who share our subjective experiences, attempt to claim victimhood, and hope what is on the table isn't using either 'truth' to build a bridge or implement medical care—and that no one tries to settle the dispute through violence."[65] Despite their somewhat disparaging language ("sect"), their argument—that when reasonable debate is replaced with vulnerability claims, the chances of achieving a compromise or just outcome diminish considerably—rings true.

I also cannot help but think that Butler is surely disingenuous when they claim that the "emergence of feminists who oppose 'gender'" is "nearly a contradiction in terms."[66] As Butler surely knows, for much of its history and in many contexts, feminists saw "gender" as the umbrella term for social roles and attitudes imposed upon and assumed to be proper to women and men, also called "sex role stereotypes," which were analyzed as a key tool of patriarchal oppression (an understanding the British Communist Party still appears to share). The concepts of "gender identity" and "gender expression"—and the idea that gender could be a generative feminist tool, rather than an antifeminist one—are both relatively recent phenomena in the unfolding story of feminism.[67] Moreover, this recent move is in some part a direct result of Butler's own work, given the massive popular influence of *Gender Trouble* in and beyond the specific, academic-activist branch of feminist studies known as gender theory or queer theory. Butler's claims of an inherent logical contradiction between the idea of feminism and a critique of gender can seem suspiciously like the willful erasure of inconvenient historical arguments and concepts via U.S. academic anachronism. In making these various sleights of hand, then, Butler sometimes sacrifices accuracy and depth of analysis—ironically, exactly what they accuse so-called gender critical feminists of doing, when writing: "If gender-critical feminists wish to be critical, then they should give some thought first to the history of the term 'critique' and its place in struggles for social transformation."[68] By accusing British gender critical feminists of a bigotry born of fear, conservatism, and transphobia, Butler collapses their motivations exactly onto those of the far right in Brazil who subjected Butler to a hateful symbolic witch-burning and direct physical attack, making two different sets of motivations and agendas appear identical.

I cannot help but note that Butler's conflated critique of gender critical feminism and the anti-gender far-right is somewhat analogous in logical structure to Peterson's critique of feminists and of "postmodern neo-Marxists" in that both authors fail to take seriously the *detail* of the positions held by those they oppose. Further, both propose a "real" or more worthy victim group (men and boys for Peterson, trans people for Butler), counterposed to a perceived "illegitimate" claim of vulnerability by the groups they are critiquing (feminists and postmodernists for Peterson, gender critical feminists for Butler). Whatever we may think of the respective merits of their claims and the stakes of their arguments, the similarity of their logic and framing is inescapable, and I argue that this is, in part, due to their shared thrall to the logic of the Tyranny of Vulnerability.

A notable difference between the strategies pursued by Peterson and Butler, however, lies in their proposed resolutions to the problems they identify. Butler states that, in place of so-called cancel culture, "we need a better conversation."[69] And in the closing pages of *Who's Afraid of Gender?*, they explicitly call for a coalition of solidarity between women's groups and trans rights movements. This would be an active alliance in the face of international far-right "anti-gender" movements, such as those in Brazil or Hungary, that are hostile to *all* forms of feminism and to LGBTQ+ rights. This is a strategy that I applaud, as it suggests a standing alongside, rather than an empathic standing in the other's shoes, the latter of which, I have argued, is often identical with a demand for a masochistic divestment of one group's own interests (an inappropriate expectation of those on either side of the debate). Peterson, on the other hand, offers as an alternative to the ills *he* spies in the current moment (the feminization of culture, the creep of so-called anti-Western values), not a gesture of collaboration, compromise, or solidarity, but instead a regression to the most sclerotic forms of traditionalism—revived myths of the male hero, Christian family values with traditional gender roles, and programmatic pronatalism (for white populations). In the cowritten collection of essays on Peterson from a leftist perspective by Ben Burgis and others, to which I am extremely indebted in this chapter, Hamilton has written: "The solution to this conundrum is not, as Peterson would have it, banally asserting the need for a rehabilitation of 'Western' values.... Rather, it lies in committing ourselves to the creation of a cultural landscape that is neither/nor—neither 'traditionally Western' in the sense meant by Peterson ... nor a mere composite of heterogeneous cultures endowed with their own respective chauvinisms."[70] It is left to one of Peterson's critical readers to suggest a third way, a strategy of compromise that echoes in some ways Butler's hopeful rhetorical gesture of solidarity in *Who's Afraid of Gender?*.

It is in light of the parallels I have highlighted above that, while not wishing to posit pure neutrality or rationality (or even pure liberalism qua Pluckrose and Lindsay) as a perfectly achievable alternative aim, throughout *Against Affect* I nevertheless seek to pursue the thought experiment of countering some of the current, commonly encountered discourses of affect that tend toward emotional blackmail with a *strategically pro-rational and pro-feminist politics*. Using the examples of Jordan Peterson and Judith Butler, we can see that, in their deployment of affect as a motor to provoke strong feeling in audiences, names on the left and the right who are in opposition to each other in the current "culture war" present, effectively, rhetorical mirrors. And, crucially, their arguments are at their weakest when emotional thrall to their own ideological affiliations guides them away from evidence.

Some Concluding Remarks

In this chapter I have examined a recent phenomenon in which the discourse of feeling is accorded a position of tyrannical hegemony paradoxically by appealing to a claim of harm, vulnerability, or victimhood that is presented as so urgent as to require capitulation to it and the denunciation or renunciation of all other viewpoints. Campbell and Manning write: "Victimhood culture is a moral framework in which victimhood has greater moral status than it does elsewhere."[71] They argue that this describes our zeitgeist. As will by now be clear, in putting forward the notion of "the Tyranny of Vulnerability" as a key facet of the affective episteme, I am in agreement with them that this describes our culture, but not with their narrow assessment of *who* deploys it and *whom* it benefits. While often lazily or cynically attributed only to the left and to the young, this discursive strategy is espoused by celebrity-hungry Lobster Kings, MAGA-hat-wearing Trump-lovers, and Hungarian homophobes, as much as by the freedom-of-expression-wary, "tender queer" campus activists, sequestered away in their safe spaces with their emotional support animals. (Caveat lector: some of these may be caricatures.) While many on the right are keen to blame identity politics and the tendency to fall back on victim claims intrinsic to its divisive structure for these phenomena, a criticism with which I have (some) sympathy, I have noted that right-wing voices are every bit as invested in tyrannizing through paradoxical claims of vulnerability as those they condemn, and that they have their own (masculinist, white-supremacist, hetero- and repro-normative, Christian family-oriented) right-wing version of identity politics—facts of which they are routinely in denial.

Drawing attention to the ways in which vulnerability is rhetorically weaponized in our culture is not intended to deny the vulnerability of any group or individual. It is crucial that we have ways of voicing distinct critiques of emotional blackmail and affective overreach in political writing and activism that do not just repeat or shore up right-wing, knee-jerk objections to *all* social justice projects. It is also crucial that we can voice these critiques without automatically being accused of bigotry or of adhering to a political or ideological position that we do not hold, simply by dint of speaking against the grain of tribalism. We need to maintain the freedom to identify and analyze such uses of language wherever they occur, and we need to view them as the building blocks of an overarching epistemic problem.

I am aware that some of my claims in this chapter—the longest and most detailed in this book—will not be popular with all readers, and, in particular, that reading Butler in parallel with Peterson to find common rhetorical logics in the way I have done may be seen as deliberately provocative. It is easy to assume that provoking is a pure pleasure, and a flippant, vacuous, and prurient one at that. But in some cases, to make a genuine provocation, as befits the title of the series of books to which I am contributing, is one of the most responsible things we may feel ourselves called to do—it is provocation as vocation. For this reason, I have judged writing critically and honestly about this hot-button issue that affects all facets of contemporary academic and cultural life so powerfully—even as I have not found it particularly a comfortable thing to do—to be a moral imperative.

4

If Reason Went Viral

Rethinking Vulnerability in COVID-19 *Culture*

*The ideology of immediacy holds a kernel of truth: we
are fastened to appalling circumstances from which we
cannot take distance, neither contemplative nor agential,
every single thing a catastrophe riveting our attention.*
—Anna Kornbluh, *Immediacy*

*Once "the vulnerable" are constituted as such, are they
understood to still maintain and exercise their own power?
Or has all power vanished from the situation of the vulnerable,
resurfacing as the power of paternalistic care . . . ?*
—Judith Butler, *The Force of Non-Violence*

*Fear is the most powerful of emotions and, as emotions are
stronger than thoughts, fear can overpower the clearest of minds.*
—Laura Dodsworth, *A State of Fear*

In my final case study of this book, I consider a range of discursive responses to the COVID-19 pandemic, all of which either enact or critically address the surfeit of affect, particularly fear, that accompanied what was perceived as a situation of global "catastrophe." I also revisit the discourse of "vulnerability" from a different perspective than that of the favored, self-adopted, and weaponized label of identity politics, as discussed in chapter 3. I consider vulnerability here as a marker that, imposed on certain citizens by public health and governmental authorities during the pandemic, denoted the relinquishment of autonomy and a capitulation to a status of helplessness—that is, a de-reasoning of a section of the population. I will examine how the category of the COVID-19 vulnerable might be understood as a recent example of how reason is distributed and a site for rethinking, resistantly, its redistribution. The redistribution of reason, if it is to mean anything, must mean recognizing as at least potentially equal to the reasoning of the lawmaker that of those abjected and othered from the category of the unmarked citizen in any given situation. The designation of "the COVID-19 vulnerable" became an exemplary "other" of our age onto whom affective attitudes (from paternalism to contempt) were projected.

In *Immediacy*, which Kornbluh notes in her acknowledgements was written during "the long lonely pandemic,"[1] she defines the immediacy aesthetic as one that, propelled by the endless circulation (of images, ideas, data) proper to late capitalism and to a hyper-mediatized age, is always already structured so as to "mimic our epidemic paths of suffering."[2] It "is a reaction to crisis that fails the bar of strategy, a reflex that is ultimately crisis-continuous." In what follows I will consider how the insistence of what Kornbluh calls immediacy harnessed to the affective episteme pushed more than ever toward affective chaos and away from resistant reason in the heightened context of the pandemic. It is the case that the contemporary fad for immediacy, as Kornbluh describes it, is perfectly suited to the ambient mood of viral transmission that characterizes a pandemic—but what if reason, rather than panicked catastrophizing or mawkish sentimentalism could instead "catch on" and put an end to the circuit of fear?

It is pertinent to note here that Sedgwick's essay in which

she lays out her understanding of the paranoid position and the reparative position, discussed in detail in chapter 1, opens with a reflection on a virus, and closes with a personal anecdote of disease. In the first paragraph, she recounts her discussion with friend Cindy Patton about the conspiracy theories circulating regarding the origin and potential racial-homophobic biopolitical deployment of HIV. (Many of these bore pre-echoes of the theories that plagued social media discourse in 2020: Was SARS-COV2 the result of a lab leak from the Wuhan Institute of Virology? Was it a racist capitalist bioweapon—a virus that eliminates the old, sick, and economically inactive, and that seemed to have worse outcomes in patients of color?) And in the final section of her article, Sedgwick muses on the life trajectories and expectancies of herself and her circle of academic-activist friends. She discusses the fact of living with advanced breast cancer at the age of forty-five (at the time of her writing), a factor that she expects will prevent her living as long as one of her close friends, then aged sixty. Similarly, two younger friends, both aged thirty, may not reach her then-milestone age, she notes, since one is living with a systemic, environmentally caused cancer, and the other is HIV-positive. Robyn Wiegman theorized in her 2014 article on Sedgwick's turn to reparation that this phenomenon needed to be understood in the light of the intimations of mortality and powerlessness she faced. And in an imitative vein, Wiegman framed her reflections on paranoia-repair around a memoir of her own attempts as a child to anticipate and interpret—and thereby somehow feel in control of—the vicissitudes of the mood variations experienced by her mother, who lived with bipolar disorder.

Sedgwick and Wiegman, then, take reflections on public and personal health crises as the spur to reflect personally on disease and to think and argue *for* affect. Conversely, in what follows, I will take the exemplary affective moment of the pandemic to make an argument for a commitment to thinking staunchly against affect, especially in times of crisis and in extremis—however difficult this may be.

Feeling Our Way Through Pandemic Vulnerability with Judith Butler

If the context of a pandemic makes perfect conditions for the outpouring of affective expression that is currently so fashionable, it is unsurprising that in their pandemic book *What World is This? A Pandemic Phenomenology* (2022) Judith Butler describes being "drawn back to phenomenology" to allow them to examine the plague world.[3] The book's title is inspired by a quotation from German phenomenologist Max Scheler: "What kind of world is this in which such a thing can happen!"[4]—an exclamation Butler finds fitting to give voice to the uncanniness and impression of impending doom that a pandemic portends. Indeed Butler states that phenomenological thinking enables them to ask questions about both experience and ethics. According to the thought of Maurice Merleau-Ponty, for example, as Butler points out, "To be a body at all is to be bound up with others and with objects, with surfaces, and the elements, including the air that is breathed in and out, air that belongs to no one and everyone."[5] Affect theoretical language, as per Butler's paraphrase of Merleau-Ponty here, tends to talk of "bodies" rather than "selves" or "subjects"—and of the body as one object among many in the world, despite Merleau-Ponty consistently hyphenating "body-subject." Affect theory can be, paradoxically, a programmatically de-subjectifying way of thinking and using language.

In *Immediacy*, as I noted in this book's introduction, Kornbluh also seeks a de-subjectified critical style by refusing to write "I." Yet, as Butler's language demonstrates here, evacuating an idea of individual self or "I" from writing is not a mechanism that ensures the enablement of critique and the escape from the affective mode, as affect can be dispersed and displaced into "bodies" or, indeed, onto "we." And, conversely, "I" can placemark a subject of singular reason. Affect, as everywhere and as the answer to everything, as panacea, does not need to say "I" to proliferate. Butler uses their phenomenological lexicon and logic to explicate what they see as the nature of vulnerability as an always already present feature of our being in the world that the pandemic exposes in a particularly stark way. They write: "We won't be able to understand shared vulnerability and interdependency unless we concede that we pass the air we breathe to one another, that we share the surfaces of the world, and that we cannot touch another without also being touched."[6] This may be true always, but Butler claims that it is strikingly and materially more salient in a respiratory disease pandemic. And Butler goes on to argue that the particular conditions of a pandemic destabilize "our usual sense of the bounded self, casting us as relational, interactive, and refuting the egological and self-interested bases of ethics itself."[7] For Butler, this self-interested ethics is one in which "we act as if our separate lives come first and then we decide on our social arrangements—this is a liberal conceit that underwrites a great deal of moral philosophy."[8] Butler offers instead a model of ethics that urges us to be aware of the always already porous and intertwined nature of our existence as a precondition for both understanding our shared vulnerability and for flourishing in society.

Notably, then, while operating in the philosophical mode Kornbluh decries, one which promotes "phenomenology as [the] limit horizon for knowledge,"[9] Butler is here targeting a similar political foe to Kornbluh's own in arguing against the "egological" self and for a commitment to the socialist collective. The one direct reference Kornbluh makes to the pandemic tellingly concerns "mask refusal as mass enactment of our nonsociety."[10]

Yet, a communistic rather than individualistic political thrust alone does not prevent affective creep or "immediacy." Indeed I would argue that this exhortation to abandon entirely the notion of ourselves as (however imperfectly) independent subjects, as "isolated individuals encased in discrete bodies,"[11] can itself pose a threat to something valuable—the self-determination that those subjects excluded from liberal reason back in the eighteenth century (women, people of color) have fought for especially hard. This is also precisely the position that those with underlying chronic illnesses or other medical contingencies (the "COVID-19 vulnerable") had to strive to achieve between accommodation of their conditions and their individual *will* to have lives worth living every day—to be more than reducible to their flawed physiology—during the heyday of the pandemic. Moreover, when chances of bad outcomes from viral infection differ at the individual level, the fact that our bodies are "discrete" *is* salient. Our boundedness as selves (however illusory poststructuralist thinking might tell us it is) matters to those labelled "vulnerable" quite a lot, because circumstances threaten every day (whether in the discourse, or in reality, or somewhere in between) to unmake those deemed *the vulnerable*, rather than the *non-vulnerable*. That experience of threat is the very core of the inchoate horror of communicable illnesses and the shadow of their supremacy during pandemic times that makes a forceful demand to be re-asserted in rational terms.

Moreover, while many cultures experience much more interconnected living than we are used to in Western nations such as the United States and the UK, a sense of the self as an individual agent, living in a society *alongside* other individuals with personal rights ending where others' begin—part of the legacy of the Enlightenment—is not a lesser or unethical way of thinking or of being. While the origins of our modern idea of "the subject" may indeed be liberal, I would insist again that this should not be collapsed onto neoliberalism—indeed the conflation of all productive notions of individuality with the negatively connoted and vaguely defined container of "neoliberalism" is a lazy and false shorthand. The conditions of the pandemic marked a crisis point as one's ability to decide upon the course of one's own life was most supremely curtailed. For some who did not fear the effects of the disease on themselves or those they loved, this curtailment was felt *only* in the effects of government-imposed lockdowns, the above-mentioned mask mandates, and social restriction measures; for those who had reason to fear both the disease *and* excessive or arbitrary government and police limitations of civil freedoms, the sense of oppression was doubled.

From Butler's perspective, then, the lessons we could take from a pandemic involve an increased understanding, and *acceptance* of, our interconnectedness-as-powerlessness as a paradoxical form of empowerment. Put crudely, they suggest that COVID-19 could make us all socialists. From a different perspective, these reflections simply highlight what was worst for some subjects about living through the pandemic—being reduced to nothing more than body-objects in the world and as little like rational selves (a rational "I") as could be imagined.

It is surprising that Butler pursues arguments that could provoke such objections in their COVID-19 book, given that some of their previous writing on vulnerability has been more critical of the concept and extremely nuanced about how it works in ways that point much more convincingly in the direction of a redistribution of reason. In the conclusion of their book *The Force of Non-Violence: An Ethico-Political Bind*—published in 2020 just as lockdown measures commenced around the world, but focusing on vulnerability in the context of questions of migration and global femicide rather than COVID-19—Butler argued that "neither vulnerability nor care can serve as the basis of a politics."¹² They recognize the individuality of the vulnerable that exceeds that label, asking, "If we think about those who, in a condition of vulnerability, *resist that very condition*, how do we understand that duality?"¹³ They also assert: "The task ... is not to rally as vulnerable creatures or to create a class of persons who identify primarily with vulnerability."¹⁴ Butler here makes two gestures. Firstly they resist the protective paternalism that can issue from an ethical understanding of the vulnerable and suggest instead something that looks like a nascent acknowledgement of a redistributed reason. Secondly they suggest avoiding the impulse to reify and make political group identities out of vulnerability (real or imagined, depending on the context) on that basis alone. Indeed they seek to ensure recognition of the continued agency and capacity for self-definition and self-determination of those deemed "the vulnerable." Butler's insights about vulnerability as political and social category here strike me as incredibly relevant to the pandemic and, in many ways, much more redolent in that context than Butler's direct reflections on the pandemic, which are deliberately located in the affective, corporeal, slippery realm of the phenomenological and directed toward an ethic of communitarianism. Thinking about COVID-19 with, and in places against, Butler forces us to think through tensions between autonomy and interdependence when imagining a category of vulnerability, between the other as threat and the other as source of connection and comfort, between our responsibility to the collective and our right to protect ourselves—and our very ability to think of ourselves as *selves* at all.

Fear and Loathing in the UK's Pandemic Management

A very different "plague book" from Butler's discussed above is journalist Laura Dodsworth's *A State of Fear* (2020), which might be described as an anti-affective manifesto for pandemic times.

Dodsworth offers an indictment of the affective manipulation carried out by the UK government (under whose jurisdiction I also lived out the COVID-19 days), its units, and other agencies during 2020 and 2021, focusing especially on the use of so-called nudge theory to seek to control the nation's behavior. It further targets the media's collusion with this project in offering resolutely grim and relentless 24/7 messaging. The principal engines of the UK government's fear propaganda were the Behavioural Insights Team (BIT), set up in 2010 under the premiership of David Cameron and colloquially known as "The Nudge Unit"—now a non-government-regulated private company—and SPI-B, a group of independent behavioral science advisors on emergencies. Dodsworth explains that "Nudges are not mandates: they are subtle suggestions, and they happen without you even being aware"[15]—a bit like the forcefield that is "affect" subtending emotions, as described by its adherents. She reports: "In one of the most extraordinary documents ever revealed to the British public, the behavioural scientists [in SPI-B] advising the UK government recommended that we needed to be frightened."[16] The wording they used is sobering: "The perceived level of personal threat needs to be increased among those who are complacent, using hard-hitting emotional messaging."[17]

Dodsworth's contention is that the UK's official pandemic response, relying on nudge theory, was exceptionally manipulative, with the result that the Brits were the most frightened and vulnerabilized nation on Earth. She notes too that nudge was used in the pandemic responses of other nations, including Canada and New Zealand, and comments that "Britain is so good at behavioural insights that we export it all over the world."[18] Dodsworth quotes the words of the woman who coined the term "nudge," Cass Sunstein: "By knowing how people think, we can make it easier for them to choose what is best for them, their families and society."[19] Dodsworth comments sarcastically: "Isn't it great that there are people who know what is best for you?"[20] Alongside the workings of the Nudge Unit and SPI-B, Dodsworth's book records how the British media programmatically ran the most alarmist and negative stories and how the daily count of cases and deaths broadcast on radio and TV led to a claustrophobic virtual prison of COVID-19 information saturation during lockdown—a perfect example of the liquid excess of "immediacy" that short-circuits rational thinking and that Kornbluh lambasts.

The response to the publication of A State of Fear, a rare call for more reason and less emotion in the pandemic, tells us much that is concerning. On the popular online discussion forum Mumsnet (originally intended for use by British parents to discuss parenting issues, but having since extended far beyond that remit and become something of a barometer of average—or "normie"—UK women's attitudes, with over eight million users), discussion of Dodsworth's book resulted in threads being removed, presumably on the grounds that it was classed as "disinformation." Mumsnet is generally known for liberal moderation policies and for allowing debate on controversial topics. For this reason, the draconian erasure of attempted discussions of A State of Fear was noteworthy. I watched this happen in real time but failed to screenshot or archive the discussions before they vanished. The only remaining evidence of their ever having appeared on the site can be found in a post on vaccine injuries from October 26, 2022.[21] A poster calling herself "DeSilvaP" writes: "Try reading 'A state of fear' (by Laura Dodsworth)." And the response comes from poster "saltedcaramel1": "If this is about to turn into a 'State of Fear #123' thread, I'm out!" Suggesting that there have been more than a hundred Mumsnet threads on Dodsworth's book is, of course, hyperbole, but it is fact that not even one of the many *State of Fear* threads that I read in 2021 still stands.

Published reviews of Dodsworth's book include a blistering account by David Aaronovitch in *The Times*. Referring to the fact that Dodsworth's previous work as a journalist, photographer, and filmmaker included a documentary called *100 Vaginas*, Aaronovitch writes, "How did a pudenda artist become a general in the rebel army?"[22] He attempts from the outset of his review to dismiss the seriousness of Dodsworth's work in *A State of Fear* by suggestively equating her earlier projects—and therefore her status and identity—with feminine frivolity. Some of Aaronovitch's objections to the book are sound: He correctly points out that Dodsworth is wrong in arguing that the method of lockdown has never before been used for pandemic management and that she seems in places to misunderstand the intentions of a vaccination campaign. But that a respected journalist reached for such tawdry, misogynistic, ad hominem attacks suggests to me a degree of outrage provoked by the very existence of Dodsworth's book that itself falls outside the bounds of these specific objections and, indeed, of rational critique. A more measured review that appeared in the *Medical Independent* agrees with Dodsworth's call for "a specific inquiry into the use of behavioural science by government," but points out that Dodsworth confuses "pandemic" and "epidemic" numerous times, gets government ministers' titles wrong, and misquotes published sources, revealing that it is a "hastily written" and "sloppy" example of journalism.[23]

While there may indeed be some inaccuracies in Dodsworth's "hastily written" book, information has since emerged directly from the WhatsApp accounts of government ministers that corroborates at least some of her findings that sowing fear in the population was a deliberate and unapologetic strategy of the UK government's pandemic response. After emerging from the jungle, where he had been appearing on the reality TV program *I'm A Celebrity Get Me Out of Here*, Matt Hancock, the disgraced former UK health minister, rushed out a book entitled *The Pandemic Diaries*. This was cowritten with journalist Isabel Oakeshott. To Hancock's embarrassment, Oakeshott turned over to *The Telegraph* screenshots of his WhatsApp messages revealing the degree of manipulation the government employed to attempt to control public behavior during the pandemic.[24] Two of the most shocking Hancock-authored messages read: "We frighten the pants of [sic] everyone with the new strain" and "When do we deploy the new variant?"[25] The mention of "deployment" of a variant is not corroboration of conspiracy theories that say the virus—and its subsequent variants—were deliberately released as a bioweapon to control the global population and prepare us for a China-style social credit system. Rather he was referring to when they should announce the spread of the newly mutated Alpha variant, which emerged in December 2020, for maximal impact. Additionally, other WhatsApp messages demonstrate Hancock and his advisors agreeing that the more pessimistic modeling should always be used in press conferences about likely case and fatality numbers with the direct aim of instilling fear, just as Dodsworth claimed.

Yet it is possible—and necessary—to note that Dodsworth's call for more reason in a situation of affective manipulation may fall short of the kind of redistributive reason I am concerned with here, and to note also that her logic fails in the face of her own prejudices. While explicitly calling for rationality rather than affect to be applied to the pandemic response, it is not, for example, a rationality that admits of the strategy of robust and individualized risk analysis in the face of health differences. Ironically, Dodsworth writes: "We seem to have forgotten that no one is safe. You have never been safe and you never will be.

Nor will I. In the blind global panic of an epidemic we have forgotten how to analyse risk."[26] While at surface level the first statement may be true, those without a functioning immune system were considerably less safe than those with one. And the second statement refuses to hear or acknowledge that those deemed the "COVID-19 vulnerable" were indeed likely to have been analyzing their risk—because the only form of reasoning Dodsworth registers is that belonging to the robust well. Dodsworth's argument here precludes redistributing reason to the vulnerable. Where her argument is at its weakest, then, is in its flawed logical deduction that, because the threat of COVID-19 was floridly deployed as an affective weapon of control, its actual threat potential was both universal and at a value of zero. Where the price of excessive affect is the paralysis of reason, the risk of excessive certainty in the infallibility of one's own reason is the arrogant underestimation of threat.

Dodsworth carries out calculations, she counts and *discounts* deaths in her book—a mechanism Butler notes as central to pandemic biopower and necropower—to reveal that "by the end of March 2021, just 689 people under the age of sixty with no co-morbidities had died from COVID-19 in England and Wales."[27] In addition to the problematic assorting of which lives *count*, Dodsworth's accountancy of harm does not even consider the prevalence of "Long COVID" and its potential effects on children and the otherwise healthy (those with "no co-morbidities")—another flaw in her logic, since these are the members of the population she would presumably consider to *count*. Moreover as Dodsworth's book was written in late 2020 and published in 2021—less than a full year after COVID-19 became known to the global population—publication was, definitionally, before the effects of Long COVID could be fully known. What we have come to understand about COVID-19 as a disease over time makes it an especially fascinating object for thinking about reason and feeling, paranoia and repair. COVID-19 can be in the worst cases a severe acute illness that, while airborne in transmission, affects many more bodily systems than just the upper and lower respiratory tracts one might anticipate. But we also now know that a mild—or even asymptomatic—case can result in severe and widespread sequelae including neurological damage. While post-viral illness is not new, Long COVID appears from current research to be uniquely devastating and concerningly common.[28] Convincing evidence that it damages the immune system—potentially permanently—is also emerging.[29] In Lukianoff and Haidt's *The Coddling of the American Mind*, discussed in the previous chapter, one of their "Great Untruths" of the cultural-affective age, "What doesn't kill you makes you weaker," turns out to be not an inaccurate overreaction in the case of COVID-19, but a literal (in the proper sense) great truth that may legitimately give us pause.

What was particularly cruel about the emotional manipulation engaged in during the pandemic was that some apprehensiveness regarding the disease may have been rational, but the governmental and media approach to it was not—at all—leading to a sense of constant low-level dis-ease. The concept of "dis-ease," often deployed in medical humanities discourse and increasingly by some physicians strikes me as especially pertinent here. In his 2004 John Boniker lecture, "Pain: Disease or Dis-ease," John Loeser traced the etymology of the hyphenated "dis-ease" back to the fourteenth century, where it was used to describe "absence of ease; uneasiness, discomfort; inconvenience, annoyance; dis-quiet, disturbance; trouble."[30] For Loeser, pain, disease, and dis-ease are intimately imbricated, and this may be a useful way of thinking about the "troubling" of our sense of normality and well-being that the pandemic caused. It strikes me that, for all Dodsworth's calls for rationality, downplaying as she does both the potential seriousness of COVID-19 and the reasoning the vulnerable were engaged in only contributes to the trend of inaccuracy for the sake of ideology that she critiques.

Kornbluh states that one of the privileged and fastest-proliferating generic forms in the era of immediacy is the first-person confessional narrative known as memoir or autofiction.[31] It is perhaps unsurprising that a number of "COVID-19 memoirs," many by frontline healthcare workers, have recently appeared and that they tend toward the emotive in tone and message. A British example of this genre is palliative care doctor Rachel Clarke's *Breathtaking* (2020), recently made into a TV miniseries, which charts her time on the hospital COVID-19 wards in the first year of the pandemic. Clarke recounts arriving home during a "Clap for Carers" session that is described as follows: "As I open the car door, applause begins to ripple and rise from my neighbours' doorsteps... And honestly, I could fall to my knees at the sound. Its kindness and sweetness and community spirit overwhelm me with raw gratitude of my own.... All these people, the passion, this trenchant solidarity. It's the loveliest cacophony in the world."[32] "Clap for carers," which began during the initial lockdown of spring 2020, was a Thursday evening ritual, during which some citizens of the UK stood outside their homes and applauded or banged pots with spoons to show gratitude for and solidarity with healthcare professionals. Laura Dodsworth speculates that this was not, in fact, the spontaneous grassroots initiative it appeared to be, but rather another nudge initiative pushed by the government.[33] Proper crises need heroes as well as villains, as Dodsworth notes, and the discourse of NHS staff as heroes or angels of the pandemic was established early on. Yet on January 2, 2021, *The Evening Standard* reported on hundreds of maskless protesters shouting "COVID is a hoax," gathered outside a London hospital—St Thomas' Hospital, the very hospital where Prime Minister Boris Johnson had been treated for COVID-19.[34] Later in the same month, *The*

Guardian reported on "COVID-19 deniers whose online activity is channeling hatred against NHS staff," resulting in a group of people being "ejected by security from a COVID-19 ward last week as one of them filmed staff, claimed that the virus was a hoax and demanded that a seriously ill patient be sent home."[35]

The reactions at both ends of the spectrum—the saccharine emotive performativity of "clap for carers" and the violent, anti-scientific, loutish protests—were equally irrational and absurd. While we were encouraged to applaud healthcare workers on doorsteps, they were not supplied with adequate protective equipment with which to do their jobs. Clarke's memoir describes the arbitrary rules around mandatory PPE use in hospitals introduced by Public Health England at different moments in the pandemic that were largely based on the varying availability of equipment, rather than on medical need. Clarke writes: "I just wanted honesty from those who rule us, sufficient COVID-19 testing and fit-for-purpose PPE. The irony, after all, could not have been lost on Boris Johnson that the one thing Hollywood scriptwriters reliably award their super-heroes is, at least, a mask and cape?"[36] By the end of 2020, The Office for National Statistics recorded 414 deaths of UK-based healthcare workers from COVID-19.[37] That they were rewarded with applause rather than with adequate personal protective equipment is, of course, both cynical and another case of weaponized sentimentality in place of effective strategy (affect over reason; immediacy over mediation).

Indeed the discourse surrounding the institution of the National Health Service (NHS), which has long held a singular, almost sacred status in British culture owing to its post–World War II welfare state values of free-at-the-point-of-use healthcare for all, was an odd one during the pandemic. A slogan to be used in TV and billboard campaigns was introduced in early 2021, shortly after the above-discussed attacks on NHS hospitals. It read, strangely, and perhaps even alarmingly: "Stay at Home. Protect the NHS. Save Lives."[38] It is noteworthy that an appeal to the emotional blackmailing Tyranny of Vulnerability discourse analyzed in the previous chapter is here deployed in the service of an institution, rather than an identity group. One would hope that the healthcare system of a nation would protect its citizens, rather than *those citizens* being called upon to protect it. As Clarke notes, "We were being asked to protect an inanimate system, not people,"[39] with the result—much documented since the pandemic—that many UK citizens stayed away from doctors' surgeries and Accident and Emergency units, resulting in excess deaths and late diagnoses of cancers that could have been treatable if caught earlier. It is hard to avoid the conclusion that the manipulation of a nation's long-standing sentimental idealization and personification of its healthcare system was deployed in a singularly harmful way here.

Similarly, the naming of Boris Johnson's "Freedom Day" in the UK, July 19, 2021—the date on which all COVID-19 rules and restrictions (facemask use, social distancing, testing and tracing) would end—was a deliberately emotive one. Researcher in propaganda Colin Alexander wrote that the label "Freedom Day" follows the rules of propaganda in appealing "to the instincts rather than the reason of the audience," and in "build[ing] around a slogan."[40] Echoing Victory in Europe Day (May 8, 1945), it further shored up the military language deployed around COVID-19, with its (expendable) "frontline heroes." Alexander notes that the concept of "freedom" is often deployed in propaganda as it connotes a positive value yet "it means whatever the target audience wants it to mean."[41] Indeed it is irresistible to note that one person's sense of liberation from restrictions, or "Freedom Day," was experienced by another person as marking their increased likelihood of contracting a virus that could seriously affect them. Butler writes: "When the economy starts

If Reason Went Viral

up following a pandemic surge, knowing full well that some people will die, a class of dispensable people is being identified and created.... It is, in fact, a rationality and a power that we must fight."[42] They hyperbolically and emotively, although I understand the impulse, describe this as "a fascist moment."[43]

A rare BBC News article in the run-up to "Freedom Day" also acknowledged this dilemma, quoting a number of UK citizens classified as clinically extremely vulnerable, including Angela, a woman with chronic lymphocytic leukemia whose vaccinations had resulted in no measurable antibody production. She voiced her perception that the COVID-19 vulnerable risked further becoming "a marginalised group in society" as "Nobody else wants their lives to be negatively affected for a minority."[44] The incompatibility between the interests of those who wanted above all to return to "normal" and those primarily concerned with infection risk represents a crisis point for the liberal "nose and fist" principle. And because the volume of the trumpeting of a discourse of triumphalist, exuberant liberationism was so loud, the reasoning of the vulnerable was largely drowned out.

Toward a Conclusion:
What Thought is Capable of in the Face of Death

By way of concluding this chapter, I will consider one further COVID-19 book: *The Plague: Living Death in our Times* (2022) by psychoanalytic critic Jacqueline Rose. Reflecting on both COVID-19 and the invasion of Ukraine by Vladimir Putin's Russia in 2022, Rose writes that "War and pandemic strip the mind bare."[45] In my introduction, I discussed how Horkheimer's belief in the force of Enlightenment values was shaken to breaking point following the evidence of the atrocities of the Holocaust. The revelation of violations of a strongly held principle or worldview can likewise apparently destabilize our conviction in reason. The outpouring of fear that surrounded the spread of COVID-19 in 2020 marked a similar moment for the crisis of reason. Rose also notes that one of the things that she found most unbearable about the pandemic was to "square what felt at the start like a new global solidarity . . . with the inequalities which slowly, or not so slowly, rose to the surface of public life, exposing the brute vulnerability of the subordinate, marginal, oppressed and the poor."[46] Solidarity turned to contempt, as explored in my previous section.

Rose opens with reflections from Albert Camus, whose 1949 novel's title she borrows for her own book, to reflect on the human inability to apprehend or offer an appropriate response to pandemic-scale events. Camus writes: "The plague was unimaginable, or rather it was being understood in the wrong way."[47] A pandemic is an event that necessarily falls outside of everyday comprehension, leading to a surfeit of emotion but requiring instead measured reason. Having laid her groundwork via Camus, I find Rose's use of Sigmund Freud and Simone Weil in the rest of her book intriguing and generative, as both are exponents of critical thinking and truth-seeking, but via unusual, nuanced, or unconventional methods—methods that might offer a better way for thinking through the pandemic and that might provide at least partial answers to some of the problems raised in this chapter.

Rose points out some of what I have alluded to in my discussion of Butler's phenomenological reading: "In a time of pandemic it rapidly becomes clear that you cannot force the world to your will. . . . Nor can you pretend that the body is within your control."[48] This awareness of vulnerability leads Rose to reflect upon Freud's last days and the late essay *Beyond the Pleasure Principle* (1920) in which he theorizes the duality of the human drives in the life instinct and death instinct, and the organism's wish to die only "in its own way." The place of human will, its relationship with reason, and their problematic complexity in our psychical organization is central to psychoanalysis and nowhere more starkly so than in that essay. I am particularly struck by Rose's reflections on Freud's death. She explains that it is very likely that Freud's physician Max Schur administered "on the basis of a spoken agreement between them"[49] a lethal dose of morphine, at the end of sixteen long years of suffering, when the pain of Freud's cancer had become more than he could bear. Rose conjectures that "Schur could only live with what he had done so long as he could trust in man's ability to subordinate his will to his reason, and—contrary, one might say, to the entire spirit of psychoanalysis—always to do what is best for himself."[50] Psychoanalysis, with its concept of an unconscious mind that deals precisely in unreason and sometimes in self-sabotage, has long complexified in a secular context the concept of an entirely free human will or capacity for perfect reason. Yet Freud's wish to be released from suffering *in his own way* speaks to the sense that a will-to-autonomy pervades our inner lives throughout times of illness and suffering, even alongside our knowledge of our own emotional ambivalences. In a state of the utmost vulnerability, reason is still possible. There is good death and bad death—death on our own terms and death that is very much not. And Rose writes, with characteristic panache, "Death in a pandemic is no way to die."[51] By engaging with these tensions in her plague book, Rose is able to explicate something Butler does not in theirs: that we value our reason, our individual agency in the world, as a mark of our dignified humanness—and that our valuing of it is not something to be sneered at or denigrated.

The book ends with an extended meditation upon Simone Weil, a fascinating and paradoxical figure who was a mystic, trade union activist, and political philosopher. Weil, as an ethicist, sought a society founded on "love for the alien"[52]—that is, a world in which common cause could be made by and with all, across boundaries of race, class, religion, health, and other status markers or group identities, in a search for radical justice. Weil described the need to imagine oneself as vulnerable and abjected, as the lowest of all subjects, if one is to engage with those in situations of abject poverty, dispossession, and persecution. And yet, as Rose notes, for Weil, there is also "something intrinsically radical in the power of thought,"[53] and she quotes from Weil: "Nothing in the world can prevent us from thinking clearly" and "nothing can compel anyone to exercise their powers of thought or take away their powers over their own mind."[54] Weil is curious in bringing together the same sort of ethical project of self-abnegation for the sake of the other that I discussed in relation to Levinas in chapter 2 (an alternative model of self-abnegation to that offered by "empathy," but that has its own limitations), and yet also a commitment to "clear thinking" and the role of a distinct "self" in possession of "their own mind." That is, Weil offers an ideal of rationality, redistributed to the most abject, *as individuals*, as a crucial element of her mercurial thought. These elements sit together intriguingly in the pandemic context and speak precisely to what redistributive reason, rather than paternalism, or coercive care, or outright altericidal contempt, might look like in extremis.

Of the accounts considered in this chapter, then, I find especially helpful Rose's endeavors to bring maverick thinkers Freud and Weil to bear on the pandemic in order to address "the question of what thought is capable of" in circumstances that both test and demand rationality.[55] Rose treads the ground between the affective overload characteristic of the discourses produced during the pandemic and a rigorous critical interrogation of them. As I have argued throughout, emotional responses are of course not always irrational or inappropriate, but when fear freezes our ability for clear thought as it did in the pandemic—and as Rose describes so convincingly in her book—and dis-ease overwhelms us, it threatens to unmake us. "Feeling" is clammy and contagious; "reason" is crystalline and pure—it stoppers the tide of fear-panic-overwhelm. One lesson we might take from COVID-19 now that we may, according to some, be entering a climate-change-fueled "pandemicene,"[56] must surely be an understanding of how to hear differing articulations of reason voiced by citizens in a culture in which redistributed reason characterizes its ethical organization and epistemological guiding force.

Rose's chosen thinkers, Freud and Weil, both do justice to the powerful nature of our unconscious and affective lives, while also stating the importance and dignity of free thought and reasoned individual will and, as shown through Weil's words, the importance of each person being deemed capable of these human qualities. While Freud is an analyst of unreason and Weil a self-avowedly anti-Enlightenment thinker, Rose shows how both offer kinds of reason that refute affective excess and that are appropriate to thinking in a pandemic. Extraordinary times, after all, call more than any other times for extraordinary thinkers.

Conclusion

For a Feminist Neo-Enlightenment

My own sex, I hope, will excuse me, if I treat them like rational creatures, instead of flattering their fascinating graces, and viewing them as if they were in a state of perpetual childhood, unable to stand alone.
—Mary Wollstonecraft, *A Vindication of the Rights of Women*

The quality of light by which we scrutinize our lives has direct bearing upon the product which we live . . . This is poetry as illumination.
—Audre Lorde, "Poetry is not a Luxury"

I do not know whether it must be said that the critical task still entails faith in Enlightenment; I continue to think that this task requires work on our limits, that is a patient labor giving form to our impatience for liberty.
—Michel Foucault, "What is Enlightenment?"

In 2020, a sculpture commemorating feminist Enlightenment thinker Mary Wollstonecraft was erected in Newington Green, North London, not far from where I live. The sculpture in silvered bronze and granite by Maggi Hambling, intended to be "for" rather than "of" Wollstonecraft, depicts a slim, muscular woman with a perfect body (according to twenty-first-century white Western beauty standards) standing atop an abstract form base.[1] Some feminists have critiqued the statue in the strongest possible terms for reducing a great philosopher to mere naked bodily matter—to her "*fascinating* graces," to cite Wollstonecraft's own words used in my epigraph.[2] After all, can we imagine anyone choosing to erect a naked statue of a man to celebrate, say, John Stuart Mill?[3] Others have defended the statue on the grounds that female nudity should not be a matter of shame. Yet others point out the anachronistic nature of the toned physique of the statue: Women would not have had sufficient access to training regimens in the eighteenth century to enable such a physique. One might, of course, argue that the muscularity of the statue's physical form is designed to stand in for Wollstonecraft's liberal muscularity of thought, that this is not a straightforwardly representational artwork. Yet the argument itself is instructive: If the only way of depicting the character of a woman's brain is by depicting a woman's body, how limited is our ideal of gendered reason, even today? How closely entwined are perceptions of women's essence and body for it to be assumed that we cannot imagine a trail-blazing female thinker without evoking the materiality of female embodiment? How far we still are from imagining, again in Wollstonecraft's words, women as "neither heroines nor brutes; but reasonable creatures."[4]

Sara Ahmed has written that "The subordination of emotions also works to subordinate the feminine and the body . . . Emotions are associated with women, who are represented as 'closer' to nature, ruled by appetite, and less able to transcend the body through thought, will and judgement."[5] The affective turn in feminism and queer theory, by raising up subordinated emotion, has arguably reified rather than challenged such assumptions—leaving intact the chain of associations:

emotion-femininity-women (and other subordinated subjects). As I have argued throughout this book, the ubiquitous deployment of a language of emotion and an elevation of the primacy of experience in both the scholarly and cultural affective turns may be understood as a "new normativity" in the Foucauldian sense of a privileged and hegemonic set of ideas that coerce by means of passing both as true and as righteous. With this understood, we may ask: What, then, is the antidote to the episteme of affect? In this conclusion, I will argue that the proper antidote is a Feminist Neo-Enlightenment, in which reason is properly redistributed. To explore this idea in more depth, I begin by turning to an essay by Audre Lorde, "Poetry is not a Luxury," written in 1977—more than a decade before Sedgwick had turned to repair and seven years before Foucault wrote "What is Enlightenment?" And I read Lorde's essay alongside that essay by Foucault.

Between the Darkness and the Light

In what is arguably her best-known essay, Lorde famously stated that "The master's tools will never dismantle the master's house."[6] By this she meant that attempting to progress, to succeed, within the terms of white patriarchal institutions, presents a feminist impasse; rather, one needs to find particular tools, specific here to the "Black lesbian feminist" experience,[7] with which to challenge the hegemony and represent difference and truth. However, in "Poetry is not a Luxury," Lorde undertakes a fascinating process of almost dialectical thinking about the concepts of "idea" and "feeling" that are central to the project I'm grappling with in this book. This process suggests an assemblage of Enlightenment thinking and traditional felt wisdom: an *adaptation* of the "master's tools." You may remember that I stated in my introduction that I am not opposed, as Foucault suggested we should be, to dialectical nuance when evaluating concepts such as the Enlightenment, or indeed affect, and being "for" or "against" them, and it was partly with Lorde in mind that I made that statement.

In this essay on creativity from the point of view of a woman of color, Lorde states: "When we view living in the european mode only as a problem to be solved, we rely solely upon our ideas to make us free ... But as we become more in touch with our own ancient, non-european consciousness of living as a situation to be experienced and interacted with, we learn more and more to cherish our feelings."[8] *Initially*, then, Lorde would seem to be undertaking a stark rejection of the mode of Western reason, associated with the tradition of the Enlightenment, and promoting instead a valorization of the realm of intuition and feeling—a pro-affect statement. Indeed Lorde explicitly states: "The white fathers told us: I think, therefore I am. The Black mother within each of us—the poet—whispers in our dreams: I feel, therefore I can be free."[9] However, what is very noteworthy throughout the essay is the extent to which Lorde deliberately uses Enlightenment language positively, and for her own ends, subtly repurposing the meaning of its imagery for her agenda.

Indeed Lorde opens the entire essay with the words: "The quality of light by which we scrutinize our lives has direct bearing upon the product which we live," and declares: "This is poetry as illumination."[10] And, a page later, she writes: "For women, then, poetry is not a luxury. It is a vital necessity of our existence. It forms the quality of the light within which we predicate our hopes and dreams towards survival and change."[11] "Light," as light shed on a problem—as illumination—is positively connoted here. However, the opposing term of "darkness" is not devalued or held as the conventionally lesser term in the binary pair. So: "For each of us as women, there is a dark place within"[12] and "These places of possibility within ourselves are dark because they are ancient and hidden."[13] The language of light and dark in Lorde's essay are deployed in ways that break down the value judgments traditionally attributed to them. "Poetry," "ideas," feelings, "light," and "dark" all subtly change status and value at different moments in the essay. The ancient and hidden dark is as important as illumination—and both are weighty. We might say that Lorde takes the symbolic lexicon of the Enlightenment to demonstrate the understanding that the language, logics, symbols, and imagery of the world in which we live shape both how we may represent our social experience and the extent to which we can forge political and philosophical change.

There are parallels in Lorde's logic with the closing words of Foucault's essay "What is Enlightenment?," which is the second quotation of this conclusion's epigraph, where he writes: "I do not know whether it must be said that the critical task still entails faith in Enlightenment; I continue to think that this task requires work on our limits, that is a patient labor giving form to our impatience for liberty."[14] Lorde is perhaps more positive and utopian than Foucault. Where Foucault states, as discussed above, that we cannot "break free" from what he calls the "blackmail" of having to be for or against reason "by introducing dialectical nuances,"[15] Lorde argues, regarding the pair of "feeling" and "idea," that "women carry within ourselves the possibility for fusion of these two approaches."[16] Lorde also states, "Women see ourselves diminished or softened by the falsely benign accusations of childishness, of non-universality, of changeability, of sensuality."[17] Here she rails against the position of the othered and calls into being an alternate imagining of "universal" that puts at the center both the *experiences* of those previously dispossessed and their right to take up the *reason* which they have been denied for too long.

The promise of a Feminist Neo-Enlightenment I espy in Lorde's essay and that I am calling for here, then, is

Enlightenment in so far as it is, pace Foucault, a "critical ontology of ourselves" that is "at one and the same time the historical analysis of the limits imposed on us and experiment with the possibility of going beyond them."[18] But it is also a form of valuing knowledge, thought, and experience that accords to women, people of color, and other nonnormative subjects the right to operate in the modes of logic and meaning-making that were withheld by the white men of history and claimed as their own birthright; it is a demand to *define ontology and epistemology*, not merely to be *affected by others' definitions*.

It is Time to Redistribute Reason Rather Than Valorize Affect

Reason—as the capacity for logic, critical thinking and challenge, agentic subjectivity, contribution to civic belonging, the motor for the action of meaning-making—is what was historically denied to the marked, the vulnerable, and the othered (those who were not white powerful men) throughout history. Emotion and a childlike lack of emotional regulation were projected onto women, onto people of color, onto people with disabilities, and onto other nonnormative subjects as an exercise of power, as Lorde so brilliantly illuminates in her essay.

The gesture of valorizing that which has been undervalued and attributed to the nonnormative is a queer reversal. And we cannot and should not ignore, as I have mapped throughout this book, that the affective turn was pioneered by queer and feminist scholars in this spirit with the best of intentions. It is undeniable that the turn to affect was both a historical corrective and a reverse discourse. But because it was, of course, never the case that women and people of color *could not* reason—it was that they were *not allowed to*, or that their reasoning wasn't *heard* as such, because reason was the name given to what was voiced by the hegemonic class of white men—the reversal did not change the cultural imaginary or political reality for the better. I have, throughout the case studies presented in this book, been putting forward the proposition that an episteme of affect rather than of Enlightenment now predominates, that the discourse of affect is often cynically deployed and weaponized, and that its currency does not, despite what may have been intended, benefit the disenfranchised and subaltern in any lasting or meaningful way. When fragile vulnerability morphed into a discourse of tyranny on university campuses, seeking to control narratives via emotional blackmail and the censorship of speech, those on the right responded with their own authoritarian affective language of threat and victimhood, as explored in chapter 3. When a viral pandemic shook our sense of physical and existential survival and instilled fear in populations, some governments and media responded with a campaign of threats, discursive terror, and irrational demands, sowing further unbearable dis-ease in the population and creating a class of the vulnerable reduced to their frail physicality and dispossessed of reason, as explored in chapter 4. These are but two examples of the failure of the episteme of affect in its cultural forms to deliver human flourishing.

In her writing on the logic of the affective turn, Ruth Leys critiqued the early affect theorists for evacuating any concern with *content* from their focus on the energy flows of affect, rendering the body of theory politically disengaged and radically empty.[19] Pace Leys, I am arguing that, when evaluating the turn to affect as a normative *cultural* mode, both form and content must matter. The rise of affect has not been a success in terms of its effects, I contend, but it has been powerfully transformative in terms of shaping our social world. It has led to an atmosphere of guilt, self-doubt, purity policing, fear of the other, and, ironically, an excess of paranoia (associated primarily with critique rather than repair by Sedgwick). So, by logical deduction, in a world in which affect is hegemonic, a novel deployment of reason must become the content and currency of the new reverse discourse.

This renewed, redistributed form of reason and its operations may look somewhat different from commonplace conceptions of the term that we take for granted and that are being promoted by pro-rationalists elsewhere, and this nuance bears more exploration. Perhaps the most strident and unapologetic recent paean to the values and triumphs of reason, science, and humanism is Steven Pinker's *Enlightenment Now* (2018). Here Pinker argues that while the Enlightenment has been an unqualified success, as he aims to show by presenting hundreds of pages of statistical data demonstrating measures of improved quality of life thanks to scientific advances, "disdain for reason, science, humanism, and progress" are prominent and growing features, not only of anti-intellectual populist movements, but also of "elite intellectual and artistic culture."[20] Pinker highlights, as I have throughout this book, that the fashion in much academic as well as broader media and political culture has turned against reason and toward feeling. He quips: "Opposing reason is, by definition, unreasonable. But that hasn't stopped a slew of irrationalists from favoring the heart over the head, the limbic system over the cortex, blinking over thinking, McCoy over Spock."[21] Yet rather than focusing on the mechanisms and false steps of the affective turn, Pinker, like those commentators discussed in chapter 3, blames with the broadest of brushstrokes "the disaster of postmodernism" tout court, with its "defiant obscurantism, self-refuting relativism, and suffocating political correctness" for this state of affairs.[22]

In attempting to persuade us of the need to re-embrace the Enlightenment, Pinker argues that it may be necessary to use a new language to do so. To this end he quotes the right-wing economist Friedrich Hayek who states: "If old truths are to retain their hold on men's minds, they must be restated in the language and concepts of successive generations." Pinker then adds that Hayek has inadvertently gone against his own point "with the expression men's minds."[23] Yet this principle appears to go only so far in Pinker's thinking too. An example he chooses to highlight that the existence of a phenomenon does not determine the form its social manifestation might take is telling: "The existence of sexual desire," he writes, does not mean "that people need Playboy clubs."[24] That the *kind* of sexual desire universalized here by Pinker is a certain flavor of male heterosexuality that *might* (but does not *need to*) result in the creation of Playboy clubs, and that "people" are elided into "men" is not, I suggest, insignificant. The default viewpoint of history's subject of reason haunts the would-be objective text. Moreover, it is noteworthy that what Hayek proposes in the quotation Pinker chooses is that "old truths" need to be *disguised or dressed up* in more palatable terms to appeal to the tastes of changing epochs, rather than that the principles underpinning valuable truths need to be argued for openly and honestly, allowing for adaptations of their forms to better fit a new cultural moment, and inviting plural contributions from those originally excluded from their construction. This too is a point on which Pinker does not pick up.

Much worse, Pinker downplays the deleterious social effects of some scientific experiments lest this undermine his argument in favor of the principle of science. He writes defensively of the infamous Tuskagee syphilis study, in which the disease progress of syphilis in six hundred African American men, many of whom were economically deprived sharecroppers, was tracked without informed consent or treatment, on the grounds that the doctors "did not *infect* the participants, as many believe" and that, therefore, the experiment "may even have been defensible by the standards of the day."[25] This logic has echoes of Laura

Dodsworth's anti-scientific refusal to accept that COVID-19 posed much threat to anyone at all, just because the public messaging about it was so emotive, as discussed in my previous chapter. Any rationality stripped of ethical responsibility in the service of scientific advancement or pure utilitarianism is not what I am arguing for here when I extol reason. And as reviewer John Gray points out in a review for *The New Statesman*, Pinker's laser focus on one kind of Enlightenment reason (the scientific) means that "Pinker's Enlightenment has little in common with the much more interesting intellectual movement that historically existed."[26] He clarifies: "Hume believed being reasonable meant accepting the limits of reason, and so too, in quite different ways, did later Enlightenment rationalists such as Keynes and Freud."[27] As discussed in the previous chapter, Freud is a rationalist whose attempt to arrive at a deep understanding of human psychology necessitated the acknowledgement and analysis of our irrational, anarchic, affective underside—without damning those qualities but also, certainly, without lionizing them, as the affect theorists do.

Moreover my own desire to see reason revalorized and redistributed is not intended to replace or elide other progressive projects. One may be concerned with redistributing wealth, or enabling social mobility, or ending global femicide, for example, *as well as* with redistributing reason; these are not mutually exclusive aims. And I would not, as Pinker appears to do in the example discussed above, assert that the end of any scientific advance, achieved by any means whatsoever, is per se justified. Twenty-first-century redistributed reason as a renewed and democratized critical mode of thinking must be primarily a way of resisting the coercive call to feel—and to feel the "right" thing, whether that be empathy, nationalistic zeal, or a virtuous display of purity politics, depending on your situatedness, your political standpoint, and the discourses to which you are exposed in the echo chambers of your world—physical and online. This book is a call to assess and to evaluate, to be ready to speak and hear dissent, to debate unpopular, uncomfortable, and controversial subjects, and to entertain plural arguments and modes of reasoning without sentimentalizing or triumphally reifying any of them.

Final Words: Mining the Past to Ameliorate the Present

Speaking in 1982, in response to a question regarding his own attitude toward the age of Enlightenment, and whether he experiences nostalgia for the "clarity" it appeared to offer, Foucault states: "All of this beauty of old times is an effect of and not a reason for nostalgia. I know very well that it is our own invention. But it's quite good to have this kind of nostalgia ... toward some periods on the condition that it's a way to have a thoughtful and positive relation to your own present. But if nostalgia is a reason to be aggressive and uncomprehending toward the present, it has to be excluded."[28] Rather than falling back on the wistfulness of nostalgia, and the human tendency to assume that things were always better in the past—that other country where they do things differently—we might take up the project of bricolage offered by postmodernism for progressive ends.

As noted, poststructuralism, often elided with postmodernism, is regularly scapegoated as the cause of what are perceived to be the negative effects of a highly affective age by some critics—often, but not always, those who lean right—without any reference to the role of the affective turn itself in shaping the direction those theoretical modes took as they entered public life and policy. In *Immediacy*, Anna Kornbluh distinguishes the stylistic mode she is critiquing from postmodernism, writing: "Where postmodernism aesthetically and epistemically embraces the surface ... immediacy mires itself in profundities of corporeality, affect, and polarized extremity."[29] I have argued for the enduring benefit of continuing to deploy some poststructuralist-originating critique in our present moment and have refuted claims that its methods are wholly incompatible with a renewed valuing of reason. And, turning to postmodernism, I am suggesting here that we may borrow its creative map of bringing together and enmeshing the ideas and theories of different moments—but without evacuating them entirely of historical and ethical context, as the most reductive tendency of postmodernism does, or putting them into urgent, breathless "circulation" without space for reasoned reflection, as Kornbluh argues against.[30] This would be in keeping with the notion of a pragmatic "tool kit," of concepts and critical apparatuses, pace Foucault. Into our neorational bricolage, we might put for starters: the Enlightenment mode's exemplary imaginative dreams of freedom—by names such as Mary Wollstonecraft and Ignatius Sancho and Phyllis Wheatley, as well as the familiar names of the white boys of the canon; Foucault's insights into reason's limitations—and potentialities; and Audre Lorde's subtle evocation of the potential power of the coexistence of previously disregarded felt wisdoms with an ideal of reason for a future feminist project.

We cannot and would not wish to go back to the original Enlightenment mode with its accompanying vicious exclusions of certain groups. And we must sit with the understanding that the "clarity" it appeared to offer was far from perfect and bears constant reclarification. We must also remember, as various writers have emphasized, that "becoming enlightened" was always envisaged as a future project, an aspirational ideal, what Derrida called "reason and its to-come, the becoming of rationalities,"[31] contrary to Pinker's assertion that "the Enlightenment has worked" and people need to be grateful for that.[32] I am in sum arguing that, in light of the reflections in this book, it may be time to usher in both a Feminist Neo-Enlightenment and something that might loosely be called a "post-affective turn," not just as another academic trend to enable the generation of ever more scholarly manuscripts (such as this one!), but as a mechanism for reevaluating the shibboleths of the past and of the present, free of the burden of faddish affective encumberments. It is time to consider what should endure in new forms for new times, what may profitably be discarded, and what, left over from a past re-viewed through an unsentimental lens, continues to matter.

NOTES

INTRODUCTION

1. Antonio Damasio, *Descartes' Error: Emotion, Reason and the Human Brain* (New York: Putnam, 1994), 14.
2. Caroline Braunmühl, *Matter, Affect, Antinormativity: Theory Beyond Dualism* (Frankfurt am Main: Transcript Verlag, 2022), 14.
3. Braunmühl, *Matter, Affect, Antinormativity*, 14.
4. See Barbara Taylor, "Feminism and the Enlightenment 1650–1850," *History Workshop Journal* 47 (Spring 1999): 261.
5. See, for example: Peter Gay, Roy Porter, and M. Teich, eds., *The Enlightenment in National Context* (Cambridge: Cambridge University Press, 1981); Peter Hulme and Ludmilla Jordanova, eds., *The Enlightenment and its Shadows* (London and New York: Routledge, 1990); Dorinda Outram, *The Enlightenment* (Cambridge: Cambridge University Press, 1995); James Schmidt, "What Enlightenment Project?," *Political Theory* 28, no. 6 (2000): 734–57; and Genevieve Lloyd, *Enlightenment Shadows* (Oxford: Oxford University Press, 2013).
6. Schmidt, "What Enlightenment Project?," 734.
7. Outram, *The Enlightenment*, 12.
8. Peter Gay, *The Enlightenment: An Interpretation*, 2 vols. (New York: Knopf, 1966–1969).
9. Lloyd, *Enlightenment Shadows*, 5.
10. Max Horkheimer, "Reason Against Itself: Some Remarks on Enlightenment," in *What is Enlightenment? Eighteenth-Century Answers and Twentieth-Century Questions*, ed. James Schmidt (Berkeley: University of California Press, 1996), 366–67.

11. Jacques Derrida, "The 'World' of the Enlightenment to Come (Exception, Calculation, Sovereignty)," trans. Pascale-Anne Brault and Michael Naas, *Research in Phenomenology* 33 (January 2003): 10.
12. Derrida, "The 'World' of the Enlightenment to Come," 20. The text he is referring to is Edmund Husserl, *The Crisis of European Sciences and Transcendental Phenomenology* [1935–36], trans. David Carr (Evanston IL: Northwestern University Press, 1970).
13. Julie Candler Hayes, "Unconditional Translation: Derrida's Enlightenment-to-Come," *Eighteenth-Century Studies* 40, no. 3 (Spring 2007): 450.
14. Jacques Derrida, *Rogues: Two Essays on Reason* [2003], trans. Pascale-Anne Brault and Michael Naas (Stanford: Stanford University Press, 2005), 159.
15. Rux Martin and Michel Foucault, "Truth, Power, Self: An Interview with Michel Foucault, October 25, 1982," in *Technologies of the Self: A Seminar with Michel Foucault*, ed. Luther H. Martin, Huck Gutman, and Patrick H. Hutton (Amherst: University of Massachusetts Press, 1988), 11.
16. Michel Foucault, *Madness and Civilization: A History of Insanity in the Age of Reason*, trans. Richard Howard (London and New York: Routledge, 2001), xii.
17. See especially H. C. Erik Midelfort, "Madness and Civilization in Early Modern Europe: A Reappraisal of Michel Foucault," in *After the Reformation: Essays in Honor of J. H. Hexter*, ed. B. C. Malament (Philadelphia: University of Pennsylvania Press, 1980), 247–65.
18. On the three essays Foucault wrote on the Enlightenment (in 1978, 1983 and 1984), and the changes of critical stance expressed in them, see Maurizio Passerin D'Entraves, "Critique and Enlightenment: Michel Foucault on 'Was is Aufklärung?,'" in *The Enlightenment and Modernity*, ed. Norman Geras and Robert Wokler (Basingstoke, UK: Palgrave Macmillan, 2000), 184–203.
19. Michel Foucault, "What is Enlightenment?," in *Ethics*, vol. 1 of *Essential Works of Foucault 1954–1984*, ed. Paul Rabinow, trans. Robert Hurley (London: Penguin, 2000), 312.
20. Foucault, "What is Enlightenment?," 313.
21. Foucault, "What is Enlightenment?," 314.
22. Foucault, "What is Enlightenment?," 313.

23. Emmanuel Chukwude Eze, "Introduction," in *Race and the Enlightenment: A Critical Reader*, ed. Emmanuel Chukwude Eze (Oxford: Blackwell, 1997), 4.
24. Chukwude Eze, "Introduction," 3.
25. Taylor, "Feminism and the Enlightenment 1650–1850," 262.
26. Margaret Jacob, "The Mental Landscape of the Public Sphere," *Eighteenth Century Studies* 28, no. 1 (1994): 106–7.
27. Taylor, "Feminism and the Enlightenment 1650–1850," 264.
28. Taylor, "Feminism and the Enlightenment 1650–1850," 264.
29. Taylor, "Feminism and the Enlightenment 1650–1850," 265.
30. Surya Parekh, *Black Enlightenment* (Durham and London: Duke University Press, 2023), 3.
31. Parekh, *Black Enlightenment*, 5.
32. Keidrick Roy, "Jefferson's Map, Douglass's Territory: The Black Reconstruction of Enlightenment in America, 1773–1865" (PhD diss., Harvard University, 2022), https://dash.harvard.edu/handle/1/37371957.
33. Keidrick Roy, *American Dark Age: Racial Feudalism and the Rise of Black Liberalism* (Princeton and Oxford: Princeton University Press, 2024), 157.
34. Roy, *American Dark Age*, 157.
35. Roy, *American Dark Age*, 174.
36. Schmidt, "What Enlightenment Project?," 734.
37. Melissa Greg and Gregory J. Seigworth, "An Inventory of Shimmers," in *The Affect Theory Reader*, ed. Greg and Seigworth (Durham and London: Duke University Press, 2010), ebook location 50–51.
38. Greg and Seigworth, "An Inventory of Shimmers," ebook location 57.
39. Greg and Seigworth, "An Inventory of Shimmers," ebook location 59.
40. Greg and Seigworth, "An Inventory of Shimmers," ebook location 68.
41. Greg and Seigworth, "An Inventory of Shimmers," ebook location 86.
42. Michael Hardt, "Foreword," in *The Affective Turn: Theorizing the Social*, ed. Patricia Ticineto Clough with Jean Halley (Durham and London: Duke University Press, 2007).
43. Patricia Ticineto Clough, "Introduction," in *The Affective Turn*, ed. Clough with Halley, 2.
44. Steven Shaviro, "Affect/Emotion," *The Pinocchio Theory*, March 3, 2016, http://www.shaviro.com/Blog/?p=1366.

45. Steven Shaviro, "Affect/Emotion."
46. Eric Shouse, "Feeling, Emotion, Affect," *MC Journal* 8, no. 6 (2005), https://doi.org/10.5204/mcj.2443.
47. Sara Ahmed, *The Cultural Politics of Emotion* (Edinburgh: Edinburgh University Press, 2004), ebook location 145.
48. Ahmed, *The Cultural Politics of Emotion*, ebook location 4833.
49. Ahmed, *The Cultural Politics of Emotion*, ebook location 4851.
50. Eugenie Brinkema, *The Forms of the Affects* (Durham and London: Duke University Press, 2014), xvi.
51. Ruth Leys, *The Ascent of Affect: Genealogy and Critique* (Chicago: University of Chicago Press, 2017), 343.
52. Leys, *The Ascent of Affect*, 344.
53. Leys, *The Ascent of Affect*, 343.
54. Dierdra Reber, *Coming to Our Senses: Affect and an Order of Things for Global Culture* (New York: Columbia University Press, 2016).
55. Patricia Stuelke, *The Ruse of Repair: US Neoliberal Empire and the Turn from Critique* (Durham and London: Duke University Press, 2021), ebook location 178.
56. Rita Felski, *The Limits of Critique* (Chicago: University of Chicago Press, 2015).
57. Stuelke, *The Ruse of Repair*, ebook location 301.
58. Anna Kornbluh, *Immediacy, or the Style of Too Late Capitalism* (London and New York: Verso, 2024), 13.
59. Kornbluh, *Immediacy*, 96.
60. Kornbluh, *Immediacy*, 64.
61. Kornbluh, *Immediacy*, 63.
62. Lisa Downing, *Selfish Women* (London and New York: Routledge, 2019).
63. Kornbluh, *Immediacy*, 196.
64. Kornbluh, *Immediacy*, 23.

1. REPAIRING WHAT WASN'T BROKEN

1. David Halperin, *Saint Foucault: Towards a Gay Hagiography* (Oxford: Oxford University Press, 1995), 122.
2. Perhaps the most explicitly Foucault-influenced queer theorist is Halperin, especially in *Saint Foucault*. Also, Eve Kosofky Sedgwick's *Epistemology of the Closet* (Berkeley, University of California Press,

1990) offers a paradigmatically post-Foucauldian reading of the workings of knowledge. The Lacanian queer trend is exemplified in different ways by names such as Tim Dean and Lee Edelman, for example in Dean, *Beyond Sexuality* (Chicago: University of Chicago Press, 2000) and in Edelman, *No Future: Queer Theory and the Death Drive* (Durham and London: Duke University Press, 2004).
3. Oliver Davis and Tim Dean, *Hatred of Sex* (Lincoln: University of Nebraska Press, 2022).
4. Robyn Wiegman, "The Times We're In: Queer Feminist Criticism and the Reparative 'Turn,'" *Feminist Theory* 15, no. 1 (2014): 4–25; Lynne Huffer, "Foucault and Queer Theory," in *After Foucault: Culture, Theory and Criticism in the Twenty-First Century*, ed. Lisa Downing (Cambridge: Cambridge University Press, 2018), 93–106.
5. Eve Kosofky Sedgwick, "Paranoid Reading and Reparative Reading, or You're So Paranoid, You Probably Think This Essay is about You," in Sedgwick, *Touching Feeling: Affect, Pedagogy, Performativity* (Durham and London: Duke University Press, 2003), 124.
6. Sedgwick, "Paranoid Reading and Reparative Reading," 129.
7. Sedgwick, "Paranoid Reading and Reparative Reading," 126.
8. Sedgwick, "Paranoid Reading and Reparative Reading," 123.
9. Sedgwick, "Paranoid Reading and Reparative Reading," 137.
10. Sedgwick, "Paranoid Reading and Reparative Reading," 137.
11. Wiegman, "The Times We're in," 5.
12. Wiegman, "The Times We're in," 5–6.
13. Patricia Stuelke, *The Ruse of Repair: US Neoliberal Empire and the Turn from Critique* (Durham and London: Duke University Press, 2021) ebook location 181.
14. Stuelke, *The Ruse of Repair*, ebook location 178.
15. Wiegman, "The Times We're In," 18.
16. Wiegman, "The Times We're In," 18.
17. Wiegman, "The Times We're In," 16.
18. Sedgwick, "Paranoid Reading and Reparative Reading," 145.
19. Kath Browne and Catherine Nash, "Introduction," in *Queer Methods and Methodologies: Intersecting Queer Theories and Social Science Research*, ed. Kath Browne and Catherine Nash (London and New York: Routledge, 2010) 4.

20. Andrew Gorman-Murray, Linda Johnston, and Gordon Waitt, "Queer(ing) Communication in Research Relationships: A Conversation about Subjectivities, Methodologies and Ethics," in *Queer Methods and Methodologies*, 112.
21. Rita Felski, *The Limits of Critique* (Chicago: University of Chicago Press, 2015), 9.
22. Robyn Wiegman and Elizabeth A. Wilson, eds., "Queer Theory without Antinormativity," special issue, *differences* 26, no. 1 (2015).
23. Wiegman and Wilson, "Introduction: Antinormativity's Queer Conventions," in "Queer Theory without Antinormativity," 2.
24. Wiegman and Wilson, "Introduction," 3.
25. Wiegman and Wilson, "Introduction," 18.
26. Wiegman and Wilson, "Introduction," 12.
27. Annamarie Jagose, "The Trouble with Antinormativity," in "Queer Theory without Antinormativity," 44.
28. Jagose, "The Trouble with Antinormativity," 27.
29. Jack Halberstam, "Straight Eye for the Queer Theorist—A Review of 'Queer Theory Without Antinormativity,'" *Bully Bloggers*, September 12, 2015, https://bullybloggers.wordpress.com/2015/09/12/straight-eye-for-the-queer-theorist-a-review-of-queer-theory-without-antinormativity-by-jack-halberstam/.
30. Wiegman and Wilson, "Introduction," 3.
31. See Lisa Downing, *Selfish Women* (London and New York: Routledge, 2019), especially Chapter 5, 128–150. On rejecting the "wave" metaphor of feminism, see Clare Hemmings, *Why Stories Matter: The Political Grammar of Feminist Theory* (Durham and London: Duke University Press, 2011).
32. Lynne Huffer, "Foucault and Queer Theory," 96.
33. Sedgwick, "Paranoid Reading and Reparative Reading," 144.

2. WHY AREN'T WE MINDING OUR OWN SHOES?

1. Hristio Boytchev, "Neuroscience or Stealth Marketing? Experts Alarmed at Free Barbies for Primary Schools to Teach Social Skills," *British Medical Journal* 382, no. 8393 (2023): 1672, https://www.bmj.com/content/382/bmj.p1672.

The neuroscience research cited by Mattel is from Salim Hashmi, Ross E. Vanderwert, Hope A. Price, Sarah A. Gerson,

"Exploring the Benefits of Doll Play through Neuroscience," *Frontiers in Human Neuroscience* 14 (September 2020) and Salim Hashmi, Ross E. Vanderwert, Amy L. Paine, Sarah A. Gerson, "Doll Play Prompts Social Thinking and Social Talking: Representations of Internal State Language in The Brain," *Developmental Science* 25, no. 2 (2022).
2. Boytchev, "Neuroscience or Stealth Marketing."
3. Frans de Waal, *The Age of Empathy: Nature's Lessons for a Kinder Society* (New York: Crown Publishing Group, 2009), i.
4. Steven Pinker, *The Better Angels of our Nature: Why Violence has Declined* (New York: Viking, 2011), 576.
5. Sharon Morrison and Frederick G. Crane, "Building The Service Brand By Creating and Managing an Emotional Brand Experience," *Journal of Brand Management* 14, no. 5 (2007): 410–21.
6. Kavya Mahajan and Mum Ghosh, "Empathy Marketing during COVID-19 Pandemic: Decoding the Impact and Effectiveness of the Brand Image," *Cardiometry*, no. 23 (August 2022): 392–98.
7. Amy Coplan, "Will the Real Empathy Please Stand Up? A Case for Narrow Conceptualization," *Southern Journal of Philosophy* 49, no. s1 (2011): 41.
8. Carolyn Pedwell, *Affective Relations: The Transnational Politics of Empathy* (Basingstoke, UK: Palgrave Macmillan, 2014), ix.
9. Carolyn Pedwell, "Affect at the Margins: Alternative Empathies in *A Small Place*," *Space and Society* 8 (August 2013): 18.
10. Pedwell, *Affective Relations*, x.
11. Paul Bloom, *Against Empathy: The Case for Rational Compassion* (London: Bodley Head, 2016), 72.
12. Maria C. Scott, *Empathy and the Strangeness of Fiction: Readings in French Realism* (Edinburgh: Edinburgh University Press, 2020), 3.
13. Peter Goldie, *The Emotions: A Philosophical Exploration* (Oxford: Clarendon Press, 2000), 8.
14. Edmund Husserl, *Phänomenologische Psychologie*, in Husserliana 9 [1925] (The Hague: Martinus Nijhoff, 1962), 321. [my translation.]
15. Karl Jaspers, *General Psychopathology* [1913], trans. J. Hoenig & M.W. Hamilton (Baltimore MD: Johns Hopkins University Press, 1997), 304.
16. Karl Jaspers, "The Phenomenological Approach in Psychopathology" [1912], *The British Journal of Psychiatry* 114, no. 516 (1968): 1315.

17. Jaspers, "The Phenomenological Approach in Psychopathology," 1315.
18. For a description of their modified concepts, see Lucienne Spencer and Matthew Broome, "The Epistemic Harms of Empathy in Phenomenological Psychopathology," *Phenomenology and the Cognitive Sciences*, August 12, 2023, https://doi.org/10.1007/s11097-023-09930-1.
19. Carl Rogers, *On Becoming a Person* (London: Constable, 2004), 34.
20. Laura S. Brown, "Empathy, Genuineness—And the Dynamics of Power: A Feminist Responds to Rogers," *Psychotherapy: Theory, Research, Practice, Training* 44, no. 3 (2007): 259.
21. Brown, "Empathy, Genuineness—and the Dynamics of Power," 259.
22. Kathleen O'Dwyer, "The Quiet Revolutionary: A Timely Revisiting of Carl Rogers' Visionary Contribution to Human Understanding," *International Journal of Existential Psychology and Psychotherapy* 4, no. 1 (2012): 76.
23. Kathryn Robson, *I Suffer, Therefore I Am: Engaging with Empathy in Contemporary French Women's Writing* (Cambridge: Modern Humanities Research Association, 2019), 7.
24. Coplan, "Will the Real Empathy Please Stand Up?," 55.
25. Clare Hemmings, "Affective Solidarity: Feminist Reflexivity and Political Transformation," *Feminist Theory* 13, no. 2 (2012): 152.
26. Andrea Lobb, "Critical Empathy," *Constellations* 24, no. 4 (2017): 595.
27. Lobb, "Critical Empathy," 597.
28. de Waal, *The Age of Empathy*, x.
29. de Waal, *The Age of Empathy*, 7.
30. de Waal, *The Age of Empathy*, 8.
31. Simon Baron-Cohen, *Zero Degrees of Empathy: A New Theory of Human Cruelty* (London: Allen Lane, 2012), vii.
32. Baron-Cohen, *Zero Degrees of Empathy*, 10.
33. Baron-Cohen, *Zero Degrees of Empathy*, 12.
34. Baron-Cohen, *Zero Degrees of Empathy*, 12. My italics.
35. Baron-Cohen, *Zero Degrees of Empathy*, 127.
36. See, for example, Peter Tyrer, "Why We Need to Take Personality Disorder out of the Doghouse," *The British Journal of Psychiatry* 216, no. 2 (2020): 65–66.

37. See, for example, Merri Lisa Johnson, *Girl in Need of a Tourniquet: Memoir of a Borderline Personality* (Berkeley: Seal Press, 2010).
38. Baron-Cohen, *Zero Degrees of Empathy*, 104.
39. Baron-Cohen, *Zero Degrees of Empathy*, 103.
40. Baron-Cohen, *Zero Degrees of Empathy*, 103. Author's italics.
41. Spencer and Broome, "The Epistemic Harms of Empathy in Phenomenological Psychopathology."
42. Spencer and Broome, "The Epistemic Harms of Empathy in Phenomenological Psychopathology."
43. See Miranda Fricker, *Epistemic Injustice: Power and the Ethics of Knowing* (Oxford: Oxford University Press, 2007).
44. Miranda Fricker, "Evolving Concepts of Epistemic Injustice," in *The Routledge Handbook of Epistemic Injustice*, ed. Ian James Kidd, José Medina, and Gaile Pohlhaus (London and New York: Routledge, 2017), 53.
45. Spencer and Broome, "The Epistemic Harms of Empathy in Phenomenological Psychopathology."
46. Spencer and Broome, "The Epistemic Harms of Empathy in Phenomenological Psychopathology."
47. Fricker, *Epistemic Injustice*, 171.
48. See Jesse Prinz, "Against Empathy," in "Empathy and Ethics," ed. Remy Debes, special issue, *Southern Journal of Philosophy* 49 (September 2011): 214–233 and Jesse Prinz, "Is Empathy Necessary for Morality?," in *Empathy: Philosophical and Psychological Perspectives*, ed. Amy Coplan and Peter Goldie (Oxford: Oxford University Press, 2011), 211–29.
49. Prinz, "Against Empathy," 230.
50. Prinz, "Against Empathy," 230.
51. Prinz, "Against Empathy," 230.
52. Prinz, "Against Empathy," 230.
53. Emmanuel Levinas, *Totality and Infinity: An Essay on Exteriority* [1969], trans. Alphonso Lingis (Pittsburgh: Duquesne University Press, 2002), 87.
54. Nai Ming Tsang, "Otherness and Empathy: Implications of Lévinas Ethics for Social Work Education," *Social Work Education* 36, no. 3 (2017): 312.
55. Tsang, "Otherness and Empathy," 314.

56. de Waal, *The Age of Empathy*, 204.
57. Tammy Amiel-Houser and Adia Mendelson-Maoz, "Against Empathy: Levinas and Ethical Criticism in the Twenty-First Century," *JLT Articles* 8, no. 1 (2014), n.p.
58. Bloom, *Against Empathy*, 5.
59. Bloom, *Against Empathy*, 31.
60. Bloom, *Against Empathy*, 24–25.
61. Bloom, *Against Empathy*, 31.
62. Bloom, *Against Empathy*, 133.
63. Bloom, *Against Empathy*, 136.
64. See, for example, Tania Singer and Olga M. Klimecki, "Empathy and Compassion," *Current Biology* 24, no.18 (2014), https://www.cell.com/current-biology/fulltext/s0960-9822(14)00770-2?_returnurl=https%3a%2f%2flinkinghub.elsevier.com%2fretrieve%2fpii%2fs0960982214007702%3fshowall%3dtrue and Olga M. Klimecki, Susannah Leiberg, Matthieu Ricard, Tania Singer, "Differential Pattern of Brain Plasticity after Compassion and Empathy Training," *Social Cognitive and Affective Neuroscience* 9, no. 6 (2014): 873–79.
65. Bloom, *Against Empathy*, 136.
66. Bloom, *Against Empathy*, 142.
67. Bloom, *Against Empathy*, 143.
68. Lobb, "Critical Empathy," 596.
69. See especially Carol Gilligan, *In a Different Voice: Psychological Theory and Women's Development* [1973] (Cambridge: Harvard University Press, 1993) and see my critical assessment of it in Lisa Downing, *Selfish Women*, (London and New York: Routledge, 2019), 102–5.
70. Baron-Cohen, *Zero Degrees of Empathy*, 29.
71. Alexis De Coning, "Seven Theses on Critical Empathy: A Methodological Framework for 'Unsavory' Populations," *Qualitative Research* 23, no. 2 (2021): 217–33.
72. De Coning, "Seven Theses on Critical Empathy," 227.
73. De Coning, "Seven Theses on Critical Empathy," 230.
74. De Coning, "Seven Theses on Critical Empathy," 227.
75. Thomas Harris, *Red Dragon* [1981] (London: Arrow, 1993), 154–55.
76. Bloom, *Against Empathy*, 2.

3. WORDS AS WEAPONS

1. Bradley Campbell and Jason Manning, *The Rise of Victimhood Culture: Microaggressions, Safe Spaces, and the New Culture Wars* (Basingstoke, UK: Palgrave Macmillan, 2018), 97.
2. Campbell and Manning, *The Rise of Victimhood Culture*, 81.
3. Robert Mark Simpson and Amia Srinivasan, "No Platforming," in *Academic Freedom*, ed. Jennifer Lackey (Oxford: Oxford University Press, 2018), 187.
4. Jacques Derrida, *Of Grammatology* [1967], trans. Gayatri Spivak (Baltimore MD: Johns Hopkins University Press, 1974), 158. For an exegesis of misunderstandings of this claim, see Max Deutscher, "Il n'y a pas de hors-texte—Once More," *Symposium* 18, no. 2 (2014): 98–124.
5. Pierre Bourdieu and Terry Eagleton, "Doxa and Common Life," *New Left Review*, no. I/191 (January/February 1992): 111.
6. Judith Butler, *Excitable Speech: A Politics of the Performative* (New York and London: Routledge, 1997), 1.
7. See Eric Heinze, *The Most Human Right: Why Free Speech is Everything* (Cambridge MA: MIT Press, 2022), 3.
8. Sara Ahmed, *The Cultural Politics of Emotion* (Edinburgh: Edinburgh University Press, 2004), ebook location 124.
9. Ahmed, *The Cultural Politics of Emotion*, ebook location 137.
10. Ahmed, *The Cultural Politics of Emotion*, ebook location 137.
11. See Marton Gera, "'Here, the Hungarian People Will Decide How to Raise Our Children': Populist Rhetoric and Social Categorization in Viktor Orbán's Anti-LGBTQ Campaign in Hungary," *New Perspectives* 31, no. 2 (2023): 104–29.
12. Daniele Albertazzi and Duncan McDonnell, "Introduction," in *Twenty-First Century Populism: The Spectre of Western European Democracy*, ed. Albertazzi and McDonnell (Basingstoke, UK: Palgrave Macmillan, 2008), 3.
13. In addition to the authors and commentators discussed in this chapter, see, to name but a few (as it would be impossible to list here all relevant commentators), publications and online content by: Peter Boghossian, Andrew Doyle, Claire Fox, Matt Goodwin, Konstantin Kisin, Douglas Murray, Brendan O'Neill, Steven Pinker, and Lionel Shriver.

14. Greg Lukianoff and Jonathan Haidt, *The Coddling of the American Mind: How Good Intentions and Bad Ideas are Setting Up a Generation for Failure* (London; Allen Lane, 2018), 6.
15. Lukianoff and Haidt, *The Coddling of the American Mind*, 7.
16. Lukianoff and Haidt, *The Coddling of the American Mind*, 7.
17. See, for example, Rosalind Gill and Shani Orgad, "The Amazing Bounce-Backable Woman: Resilience and the Psychological Turn in Neoliberalism," *Sociological Research Online* 23, no. 2 (2018): 477–95.
18. Helen Pluckrose and James Lindsay, *Cynical Theories: How Activist Scholarship Made Everything about Race, Gender and Identity—and Why this Harms Everybody* (London: Swift, 2020), 12.
19. Pluckrose and Lindsay, *Cynical Theories*, 12.
20. Pluckrose and Lindsay, *Cynical Theories*, 12.
21. See: Lisa Downing, *Selfish Women*, (London and New York: Routledge, 2019), especially Chapter 5, 128–50; Lisa Downing, "The Body Politic: Gender, The Right Wing and 'Identity Category Violations,'" *French Cultural Studies* 29, no. 4 (2018): 367–77.
22. Pluckrose and Lindsay, *Cynical Theories*, 237.
23. Pluckrose and Lindsay, *Cynical Theories*, 209.
24. Susan Neiman, *Left Is Not Woke* (Cambridge: Polity, 2023), 14.
25. Neiman, *Left Is Not Woke*, 18.
26. Neiman, *Left Is Not Woke*, 16.
27. Neiman, *Left Is Not Woke*, 16.
28. Neiman, *Left Is Not Woke*, 145.
29. Samuel C. Huneke, "Critically Cringe: On Susan Neiman's *Left Is Not Woke*." *Los Angeles Review of Books*, September 17, 2023, https://lareviewofbooks.org/article/critically-cringe-on-susan-neimans-left-is-not-woke/.
30. See: "Letter to the Editor: Response from Susan Neiman on *Left Is Not Woke*," *Los Angeles Review of Books*, October 8, 2023, https://lareviewofbooks.org/article/letter-to-the-editor-response-from-susan-neiman-on-left-is-not-woke/. The quotations are from Neiman, *Left Is Not Woke*, 11.
31. Neiman, *Left Is Not Woke*, 60.
32. Lisa Downing, "Author Functions and Freedom: 'Michel Foucault' and 'Ayn Rand' in the Anglophone 'Culture Wars.'" *Paragraph* 46, no. 3 (2023): 279–89.

33. Samuel C. Huneke, "Critically Cringe: On Susan Neiman's *Left Is Not Woke*."
34. Wendy Brown, *States of Injury: Power and Freedom in Late Modernity* (Princeton: Princeton University Press, 1995).
35. For an account of why Peterson may have misunderstood the implications of the bill, see Josh Taylor, "What is in a Name? A Response to Jordan Peterson's Critiques of Pronoun Regulations and Free Speech Laws," *Oxford Political Review*, April 21, 2019, https://oxfordpoliticalreview.com/2019/04/21/what-is-in-a-name-a-response-to-jordan-petersons-critiques-of-pronoun-regulations-and-free-speech-laws/.
36. Ben Burgis, "On Lobsters, Logic and the Pitfalls of Good Rhetoric," in *Myth and Mayhem: A Leftist Critique of Jordan Peterson*, ed. Ben Burgis, Conrad Hamilton, Matthew McManus, and Marion Trejo (Winchester and Washington: Zero Books, 2020), 209.
37. Slavoj Žižek, "Jordan Peterson as a Symptom . . . of What? The Art of Lying with Truth," in *Myth and Mayhem*, 1.
38. Martha Nussbaum, "The Professor of Parody: The Hip Defeatism of Judith Butler," *The New Republic*, February 22, 1999, https://newrepublic.com/article/150687/professor-parody.
39. Judith Butler, *Who's Afraid of Gender?* (Harmondsworth, UK: Penguin, 2024).
40. Jordan Peterson, *12 Rules for Life: An Antidote to Chaos* (London: Allen Lane, 2018), 14.
41. Peterson, *12 Rules for Life*, xxviii.
42. Peterson, *12 Rules for Life*, 324. My italics.
43. Kate Manne, "Reconsider the Lobster," *Times Literary Supplement*, May 25, 2018.
44. Žižek, "Jordan Peterson as a Symptom . . . of What?," 13.
45. Peterson, *12 Rules for Life*, 330.
46. Marion Trejo, "On Peterson's Anti-Feminism," in *Myth and Mayhem*, 208.
47. Trejo, "On Peterson's Anti-Feminism," 208.
48. Intelligence Squared, podcast, May 24, 2018, https://www.youtube.com/watch?v=7QRQjrsFnR4.
49. Cited in Conrad Hamilton, "Peterson's Reckoning with the Left," in *Myth and Mayhem*, 167.

50. Hamilton, "Peterson's Reckoning with the Left," 168.
51. Hamilton, "Peterson's Reckoning with the Left," 176.
52. Butler, *Who's Afraid of Gender?*, 289.
53. See Brock Colyar, "Gender Troubled: Judith Butler's Culture War Misfire," *The Drift*, no. 12, March 5, 2024, https://www.thedriftmag.com/gender-troubled/.
54. Colyar, "Gender Troubled: Judith Butler's Culture War Misfire."
55. Keith Contorno, "Fighting the Phantom in *Who's Afraid of Gender?*," *Chicago Review of Books*, March 19, 2024, https://chireviewofbooks.com/2024/03/28/whos-afraid-of-gender/.
56. Butler, *Who's Afraid of Gender?*, 4.
57. Butler, *Who's Afraid of Gender?*, 134.
58. Sarah Lamble, "Confronting Complex Alliances: Situating Britain's Gender Critical Politics within the Wider Transnational Anti-Gender Movement," *Journal of Lesbian Studies* 28, no. 3 (2024), 504–17.
59. Lamble, "Confronting Complex Alliances," 505.
60. Butler, *Who's Afraid of Gender?*, 135.
61. See "The Gender Recognition Bill and Equality Law," News, Communist Party UK, published March 2023, https://www.communistparty.org.uk/the-gender-recognition-bill-and-equality-law/.
62. Darren Langdridge, *Sexual Citizenship and Social Change: A Dialectical Approach to Narratives of Tradition and Critique* (Oxford: Oxford University Press, 2024), 94.
63. Keith Contorno, "Fighting the Phantom in *Who's Afraid of Gender?*."
64. Pluckrose and Lindsay, *Cynical Theories*, 209.
65. Pluckrose and Lindsay, *Cynical Theories*, 250.
66. Butler, *Who's Afraid of Gender?*, 134.
67. See Lucy Nichols and Sal Clark, "Gender, Sex and Freedom: Testing the Theoretical Limits of the Twenty-First-Century 'Gender Wars' with Simone de Beauvoir, Shulamith Firestone and Luce Irigaray," *Paragraph* 46, no. 3 (2013), 354–71.
68. Butler, *Who's Afraid of Gender?*, 141.
69. Butler, *Who's Afraid of Gender?*, 150.
70. Hamilton, "Peterson's Reckoning with the Left," 132.
71. Campbell and Manning, *The Rise of Victimhood Culture*, 105.

4. IF REASON WENT VIRAL

1. Anna Kornbluh, *Immediacy, or the Style of Too Late Capitalism* (London and New York: Verso, 2024).
2. Kornbluh, *Immediacy*, 47.
3. Judith Butler, *What World is This? A Pandemic Phenomenology* (New York: Columbia University Press, 2022), 17.
4. Butler, *What World is This?*, 17.
5. Butler, *What World is This?*, 37.
6. Butler, *What World is This?*, 12.
7. Butler, *What World is This?*, 12.
8. Butler, *What World is This?*, 41.
9. Kornbluh, *Immediacy*, 96.
10. Kornbluh, *Immediacy*, 9.
11. Butler, *What World is This?*, 38.
12. Judith Butler, *The Force of Non-Violence: An Ethico-Political Bind* (London and New York: Verso, 2020), 183.
13. Butler, *The Force of Non-Violence*, 184. My italics.
14. Butler, *The Force of Non-Violence*, 184.
15. Laura Dodsworth, *A State of Fear: How the UK Government Weaponised Fear During the COVID-19 Pandemic* (London: Pinter & Martin, 2021), 60.
16. Dodsworth, *A State of Fear*, 2.
17. Dodsworth, *A State of Fear*, 2.
18. Dodsworth, *A State of Fear*, 61.
19. Dodsworth, *A State of Fear*, 60.
20. Dodsworth, *A State of Fear*, 60.
21. See EmmaH2022, "Hope okay to put this here—mandates," Mumsnet, https://www.mumsnet.com/talk/coronavirus/4663938-hope-okay-to-put-this-here-mandates?page=2.
22. David Aaronovitch, "*A State of Fear* by Laura Dodsworth: Review—A Covidiot's Guide to The Pandemic," *The Times*, June 11, 2021, https://www.thetimes.com/culture/books/article/a-state-of-fear-how-the-uk-government-weaponised-fear-during-the-covid-19-pandemic-by-laura-dodsworth-review-zgww3tf82.
23. "A hastily written, sloppy book that fails to convince," Mindo, *Medical Independent*, December 7, 2021, https://www.medicalindependent.ie/life/a-hastily-written-sloppy-book-that-fails-to-convince/.

24. See the dossier at "The Lockdown Files," *The Telegraph*, https://www.telegraph.co.uk/news/lockdown-files/.
25. See Nadeem Badshah, "Matt Hancock Wanted to 'Frighten Everyone' into Following COVID Rules," *The Guardian*, March 5, 2023, https://www.theguardian.com/politics/2023/mar/05/matt-hancock-wanted-to-frighten-everyone-into-following-covid-rules.
26. Dodsworth, *A State of Fear*, 269.
27. Dodsworth, *A State of Fear*, 5.
28. See, for a small exemplary sample, Hannah E. Davis, Gina S. Assaf, Lisa McCorkell, et al., "Characterizing Long COVID in an International Cohort: 7 Months of Symptoms and their Impact," *EClinicalMedicine* 38 (August 2021), https://www.thelancet.com/action/showPdf?pii=S2589-5370%2821%2900299-6; Hanson Global Burden of Disease Long COVID Collaborators, "Estimated Global Proportions of Individuals with Persistent Fatigue, Cognitive, and Respiratory Symptom Clusters Following Symptomatic COVID-19 in 2020 and 2021," *The Journal of the American Medical Association* 328, no. 16 (2022), 1604–15; Trisha Greenhalgh, Manoj Sivan, Alice Perlowski, and Janko Ž. Nikolich, "Long COVID: A Clinical Update," *Lancet* 404, no. 10453 (2024), 707–24.
29. See, for example, Chetan Sharm and Jagadeesh Bayry, "High Risk of Autoimmune Diseases after COVID-19," *National Review of Rheumatology* 19, no. 7 (2023): 399–400.
30. John D. Loeser, "Pain: Disease or Dis-ease? The John Bonica Lecture: Presented at the Third World Congress of World Institute of Pain, Barcelona 2004," *Pain Practice* 5, no. 2 (2005): 79.
31. Kornbluh, *Immediacy*, 69.
32. Rachel Clarke, *Breathtaking: Inside the NHS in a Time of Pandemic* (London: Little, Brown, 2021), 156. Adapted as *Breathtaking*, an ITV dramatization of Rachel Clarke's memoir, written by Jed Mercurio, Rachel Clarke and Prasanna Puwanajarah, directed by Craig Viveiros, 2024.
33. Dodsworth, *A State of Fear*, 97.
34. Michael Howie, "Doctor Tells of 'Heartbreak' as Crowd Shouted 'COVID is a Hoax' outside St Thomas' Hospital," *The Standard*, January 2, 2021, https://www.standard.co.uk/news/london/doctor-covid-hoax-crowd-outside-st-thomas-hospital-b633377.html.

35. Ben Quinn and Denis Campbell, "Hospital Incursions by COVID Deniers Putting Lives at Risk, Say Health Leaders," *The Guardian*, January 27, 2021, https://www.theguardian.com/world/2021/jan/27/hospital-incursions-by-covid-deniers-putting-lives-at-risk-say-leaders.
36. Clarke, *Breathtaking*, 206.
37. ONS data on COVID deaths can be found here: https://www.ons.gov.uk/peoplepopulationandcommunity/healthandsocialcare/conditionsanddiseases.
38. See "New TV Advert Urges Public to Stay at Home to Protect the NHS and Save Lives," Press Release, Gov.UK, published January 10, 2021, https://www.gov.uk/government/news/new-tv-advert-urges-public-to-stay-at-home-to-protect-the-nhs-and-save-lives.
39. Clarke, *Breathtaking*, 189.
40. Colin Alexander, "Why Freedom Day is the Latest Example of COVID Propaganda," *The Conversation*, July 18, 2021, https://theconversation.com/why-freedom-day-is-the-latest-example-of-covid-propaganda-164521.
41. Alexander, "Why Freedom Day is the Latest Example of COVID Propaganda."
42. Butler, *What World is This?*, 93.
43. Butler, *What World is This?*, 93.
44. Joseph Lee and Francesca Gillett, "COVID-19: 'For Us It's Not Freedom Day, Is It?,'" *BBC News*, 6 July, 2021, https://www.bbc.co.uk/news/uk-57643063.
45. Jacqueline Rose, *The Plague: Living Death in Our Times* (London: Fitzcarraldo Editions, 2023), 37.
46. Rose, *The Plague*, 7.
47. Rose, *The Plague*, 19.
48. Rose, *The Plague*, 70.
49. Rose, *The Plague*, 46.
50. Rose, *The Plague*, 46.
51. Rose, *The Plague*, 49.
52. Cited in Rose, *The Plague*, 15.
53. Rose, *The Plague*, 17.
54. Cited in Rose, *The Plague*, 17.
55. Rose, *The Plague*, 16.

56. See, for example, the interview with Ed Yong for *Democracy Now*: "'We Created the Pandemicene': Ed Yong on How the Climate Crisis Could Spark the Next Pandemic," *Democracy Now*, April 29, 2023, https://www.democracynow.org/2022/4/29/ed_yong_p.

CONCLUSION

1. Eleanor Nairne, "A Naked Statue for a Feminist Hero?," *New York Times*, November 12, 2020, https://www.nytimes.com/2020/11/12/arts/design/mary-wollstonecraft-statue-london.html?fbclid=Iwar0ycQmaYas2bIqdDs7upAtYstcLz3jeOvmqrl1qgwple6tvyyqQ/dsl09ro.
2. Mary Wollstonecraft, *A Vindication of the Rights of Women, With Strictures on Political and Moral Subjects* [1792] (Minneola NY: Dover, 1996), 4.
3. See: Rhiannon Lucy Cosslett, "Why I Hate the Mary Wollstonecraft Statue: Would a Man be 'Honoured' with his Schlong Out?," *The Guardian*, November 10, 2020, https://www.theguardian.com/artanddesign/2020/nov/10/why-i-hate-the-mary-wollstonecraft-statue.
4. Wollstonecraft, *Vindication of the Rights of Women*, 134.
5. Sara Ahmed, *The Cultural Politics of Emotion* (Edinburgh: Edinburgh University Press, 2004), ebook location 111.
6. Audre Lorde, "The Master's Tools Will Never Dismantle the Master's House," in *The Master's Tools Will Never Dismantle the Master's House* (Harmondsworth: Penguin Modern, 2018), 16–21.
7. Lorde, "The Master's Tools Will Never Dismantle the Master's House," 16.
8. Audre Lorde, "Poetry is not a Luxury," in *The Master's Tools Will Never Dismantle the Master's House*, 2.
9. Lorde, "Poetry is not a Luxury," 4.
10. Lorde, "Poetry is not a Luxury," 1.
11. Lorde, "Poetry is not a Luxury," 2.
12. Lorde, "Poetry is not a Luxury," 1.
13. Lorde, "Poetry is not a Luxury," 1.
14. Michel Foucault, "What is Enlightenment?," in *Ethics*, vol. 1 of *Essential Works of Foucault 1954–1984*, ed. Paul Rabinow, trans. Robert Hurley (London: Penguin, 2000), 319.

15. Foucault, "What is Enlightenment?," 313.
16. Lorde, "Poetry is not a Luxury," 2.
17. Lorde, "Poetry is not a Luxury," 3.
18. Foucault, "What is Enlightenment?," 319.
19. Ruth Leys, *The Ascent of Affect: Genealogy and Critique* (Chicago: University of Chicago Press, 2017), 343.
20. Steven Pinker, *Enlightenment Now: The Case for Reason, Science, Humanism, and Progress* (London and New York: Penguin, 2018), 29.
21. Pinker, *Enlightenment Now*, 351.
22. Pinker, *Enlightenment Now*, 406.
23. Pinker, *Enlightenment Now*, 5.
24. Pinker, *Enlightenment Now*, 431.
25. Pinker, *Enlightenment Now*, 401.
26. John Gray, "Unenlightened Thinking: Steven Pinker's Embarrassing New Book is a Feeble Sermon for Rattled Liberals," *The New Statesman*, February 22, 2018, https://www.newstatesman.com/culture/2018/02/enlightenment-now-the-case-for-reason-science-humanism-and-progress-review-steven-pinker.
27. Gray, "Unenlightened Thinking."
28. Rux Martin and Michel Foucault, "Truth, Power, Self: An Interview with Michel Foucault, October 25, 1982," in *Technologies of the Self: A Seminar with Michel Foucault*, ed. Luther H. Martin, Huck Gutman, and Patrick H. Hutton (Amherst: University of Massachusetts Press, 1988), 12.
29. Anna Kornbluh, *Immediacy, or the Style of Too Late Capitalism* (London and New York: Verso, 2024), 13.
30. Kornbluh, *Immediacy*, 69.
31. Jacques Derrida, "The 'World' of the Enlightenment to Come (Exception, Calculation, Sovreignty)." Trans. Pascale-Anne Brault and Michael Naas. *Research in Phenomenology* 33 (2003): 27. See also: Dorindra Outram, *The Enlightenment* (Cambridge: Cambridge University Press, 1995), 1; Surya Parekh, *Black Enlightenment* (Durham and London: Duke University Press, 2023), 5; Genevieve Lloyd, *Enlightenment Shadows* (Oxford: Oxford University Press, 2013).
32. Pinker, *Enlightenment Now*, 6.

IN THE PROVOCATIONS SERIES

Who Would You Kill to Save the World?
Claire Colebrook

Hatred of Sex
Oliver Davis and Tim Dean

Against Affect
Lisa Downing

Declarations of Dependence: Money, Aesthetics, and the Politics of Care
Scott Ferguson

The People Are Missing: Minor Literature Today
Gregg Lambert

I'm Not Like Everybody Else: Biopolitics, Neoliberalism, and American Popular Music
Jeffrey T. Nealon

Abolishing Freedom: A Plea for a Contemporary Use of Fatalism
Frank Ruda

Dirty Knowledge: Academic Freedom in the Age of Neoliberalism
Julia Schleck

The Earth Is Evil
Steven Swarbrick

Contra Instrumentalism: A Translation Polemic
Lawrence Venuti

Free Listening
Naomi Waltham-Smith

To order or obtain more information on these or other University of Nebraska Press titles, visit nebraskapress.unl.edu.

www.ingramcontent.com/pod-product-compliance
Lightning Source LLC
Chambersburg PA
CBHW030115170426
43198CB00009B/632